John Llewelyn Davies

The Gospel and modern life

John Llewelyn Davies
The Gospel and modern life
ISBN/EAN: 9783337282868
Printed in Europe, USA, Canada, Australia, Japan
Cover: Foto ©Thomas Meinert / pixelio.de

More available books at **www.hansebooks.com**

BY THE
REV. J. LLEWELYN DAVIES, M.A.
RECTOR OF CHRIST CHURCH, ST MARYLEBONE.

SECOND EDITION.

London:
MACMILLAN AND CO.
1875.

THE present volume includes, together with the Sermons entitled "The Gospel and Modern Life," a short course delivered at Cambridge in the year 1867, on the names Eucharist, Sacrifice, and Communion, and published separately under the title of "Morality according to the Sacrament of the Lord's Supper."

CONTENTS.

	PAGE
PREFACE	vii

SERMON I.
THE KINGDOM OF CHRIST AND THE CHURCH . . . 1

SERMON II.
THE KINGDOM OF CHRIST AND THE CHRISTIAN . . 14

SERMON III.
THE KINGDOM OF CHRIST AND THE WORLD . . 27

SERMON IV.
CHRIST AND MODERN KNOWLEDGE . . 41

SERMON V.
HUMANITY AND THE TRINITY. . . . 58

SERMON VI.
NATURE 72

SERMON VII.
RELIGION 87

SERMON VIII.
THE CONSCIENCE 101

	PAGE
Human Corruption	115

SERMON X.
Human Holiness	129

SERMON XI.
Lives of the Saints	142

SERMON XII.
Common Worship	156

SERMON XIII.
Preaching	171

SERMON XIV.
Giving by Calculation	183

SERMON XV.
Public and Private Expenditure	197

SERMON XVI.
The Irish Church Question	211

DISCOURSE I.
The Eucharist	226

DISCOURSE II.
Sacrifice	245

DISCOURSE III.
Communion	266

PREFACE TO THE FIRST EDITION OF "THE GOSPEL AND MODERN LIFE," 1869.

THE *Pall Mall Gazette*, besides its other claims on public attention, has distinguished itself by taking a decided line in matters relating to theology. The conductors of this newspaper have declined to regard theology as a province with which the general public has nothing to do, and have had the candour, whilst they attack the religious professions of others, to enunciate in vigorous and plain-spoken writing a creed of their own. They thus address a fair challenge to those whose creed they assail, and in one of their recent criticisms they have made it especially incumbent upon those who hold such a faith as is set forth in this volume to consider what reason they can give for their hope.

The first article in the creed of the *Pall Mall Gazette* is, that as to things belonging to the unseen world certainty is not to be attained. Some suppositions are probable. Nothing is more than probable. To this preliminary article the *Gazette* returns again and again. Amongst probable suppositions in the sphere of religion these are the three which specially commend themselves,—the existence of a God, a future state, rewards and punishments awaiting virtue and vice. Many arguments point to these as probable; and a rational man will at the same time guard himself from assuming their certainty and allow himself to be swayed by their probability. But every form of systematic theology must be surrendered. For "as soon as you admit that probability is the utmost to which you can attain upon these subjects, it becomes plain that the uncertainty of every inference which you draw increases in a geometrical ratio." Accordingly on one Easter Eve (1867) the writer whose voice is to be chiefly heard in the theology of the *Pall Mall Gazette*, protested that the keeping of Good Friday and Easter Day was an obsolete superstition. The death and resurrection of Jesus Christ were not to him historical facts which it was worth while to remember. He did not care to have these in any sense brought before him.

There are many, it must be admitted, who similarly renounce all grateful commemoration of the life of Christ. But what is very singular in this writer is that he nevertheless thinks it well to go to Church. He introduces a representative of his opinions as saying, "I attend public worship, because I thoroughly believe it to be a good thing." How he would reconcile the acceptance of any form of Christian service with the repudiation of Good Friday and Easter Day he does not explain.

He only declares that his custom of going to Church agrees exactly with his state of mind, and that his state of mind is rational, decided, and contented. I should have thought that such acquiescence as is expressed in going to Church would have covered the special observation of the Death and Resurrection on which all Christian worship is founded. But it is at least evident that there might be a more suitable "expression for the great suppositions" mentioned above than prayers offered in the name of Christ to the Father. The liturgy in which this writer would rationally unite with his fellow-believers would be something to this effect: "O God, if there be a God (of which I am by no means sure, and insist positively that no one else shall be sure), I consider it highly probable (but not, I emphatically insist, more than probable), that virtue will be rewarded and vice punished. I intend therefore to cultivate virtue." But those who could adopt this confession of faith do not generally think it worth while to come together solemnly for the purpose of uttering it.

This, the writer contends, is not scepticism. It is to be "in a state of enforced and therefore contented ignorance on most of the great topics of religion." According to him, the ship of our life is "one upon which the sun never shines." Certainly this state of mind is a different one from that which we commonly call sceptical. The writer is entitled to protest against loose charges of scepticism, atheism, infidelity, being thrown against a creed so well defined and so consistently supported as this to which the *Pall Mall Gazette* has given its adhesion. Thinkers who have come to a stand a little on the other side of Deism, and make that contentedly their resting-place, ought on every ground to be distinguished from the larger class, properly described as sceptical, who waver between moods of belief and of doubt. These are in the better or the worse condition of not knowing thoroughly their own minds. There is a profounder doubt than that of the *Pall Mall Gazette*, and a larger faith, which have conflicting attractions more powerful than those of any *juste milieu* of Deism. On the one hand there is a hope of being rid of endless difficulties, if we once make a clean sweep and resolve to know neither a God nor a future life. We might still agree to cultivate virtue as that which promotes the general well-being; but why trouble ourselves with these questions which reach out into the unknown, and which we can never satisfactorily solve? Deism, however unimpassioned and calculating, leaves one a prey to all the most difficult problems by which the human mind has been vexed. On the other hand, no one denies—hardly any one is insensible to—

the attractions of the Christian Faith. Many have wished they could be devout Christians, even when inquiry has seemed to make it impossible. It is true, as we should be quickly reminded in the *Pall Mall Gazette*, that the question for a sensible man is not what is attractive, but what is rational. But I am now speaking, not of what is pleasant, but of what draws and prevails upon the reason. And it is not too much to say that there are innumerable considerations, of varying degrees of power, which might seem to any man when he gives his mind to them—not to befool him into being a Christian, but—to make it unreasonable for him not to be a Christian. It is not wonderful, therefore, that a great deal of simple uncertainty should prevail as to the foundations on which men in these days may build their lives, and the hopes by which their efforts may be inspired. I do not take upon me to say that those who, upon the whole, have resolved to believe nothing about the unseen world cannot secure themselves absolutely against misgivings; but it must in candour be admitted that loyal and devout Christians, now as always,— for the personal history of the most zealous champions of the faith shews that this has been their common experience,—have times when the very things that they live by seem questionable and unreal to them.

Christians in general, therefore, would oppose to such a creed as that of the *Pall Mall Gazette*, not the pretence of conclusions which they can demonstrate against all comers, but strong and deep convictions continually assailed and sometimes agitated by insoluble difficulties. These difficulties are especially formidable to those who mix with the world, and to those who study with interest the progress of thought in the provinces of natural science and historical criticism. And the question which they have to ask themselves is whether their convictions as to the nature of God and the work of reconciliation are of such a kind, and rest upon such a ground, that they do right in saying, 'I cannot fully answer this or that objection, nevertheless I will persevere in believing.' And then it must come into view that the arguments by which Christians of the firmest faith are and have been always most powerfully moved are not such as it is easy to lay out in controversy, or such as can be conveniently weighed or measured by logical instruments. One way of describing them is to say that they are such as verify the Christian hypothesis, which is, that there is a living God, acting upon the spirits of men, and seeking to draw them by the proper influences to a supersensual life of faith and love. Christians are continually tempted to do what all controversy solicits them to do, namely, to forget their hypothesis, and to argue as if their business was to establish, in the light of the understanding, certain conclusions to which every rational person must assent. But this is to put the main point, the attractive action of God himself, out of the question. If the end of God be what we hold it to be, to bring human souls to himself, then the means he actually employs must be living and spiritual. They are likely to be infinitely various and subtle, but they will deal principally with the conscience and the affections. God is likely—nay, is certain—to manifest himself more and more in proportion to faith and love. Christian appeals belong naturally to a region that may be called mystical, or may be otherwise described as personal and spiritual. The experience of the inner life, rightly understood and tested, is the best evidence that can be adduced. Words which one man can say out of his heart may strongly move another man. If we will not acknowledge evidence of this kind, the evidence does not perish or lose its power, but we are simply remaining on the outside of the question.

No Christian need be ashamed of trying to rise into the sphere of those motives and to submit to the government of those influences which have produced all that is best in Christendom. But the truth is that no one, Christian or non-Christian, can become serious and think of what he himself lives by and for, without appealing to considerations which may incur the taunt of being personal and mystical.

The writer whom I am now criticizing appears to me to be himself not exempt from the weakness which he despises in others. The *Pall Mall Gazette* contained not long since two articles of striking ability discussing the grounds of religious belief. The first of these (Oct. 17th, 1868) was a review of a tract by Mr Thos. Hughes, originally published in the series called *Tracts for Priests and People*. The review was aimed at the school to which Mr Hughes belongs. "If we are asked why we have given so much space to this performance, our answer is that it is a representative tract. It illustrates the effect upon a man of standing and talent of a school which we think is rapidly losing its influence, but which in its day threw numbers of promising men upon a hopelessly false scent in matters of the utmost importance.... Mr Hughes shews its characteristics in the most naked form.... He considers that the great question about every creed proposed to men is not whether it is true but whether it 'answers,'—whether, that is, those who have been brought up in it like it." Mr Hughes's tract was entitled *A Layman's Faith*. The intention of it was to give his own personal convictions and experience for what they were worth. It may be presumed that he felt the reluctance of a modest and reverent nature to speak about himself; but he thought it right to overcome that reluctance and to profess himself to be a believer, with his whole heart and mind, in the simple Gospel of Christ. His faith, so he told those who cared to hear him, was not a thing worn lightly, but was rooted in his deepest convictions. So personal a statement as that of Mr Hughes, requires, most persons will think, to be justified by peculiar circumstances. But his reviewer raises no question about the taste or discretion of the tract; he does not accuse the writer of egregious vanity or assumption. His objection is to the notion that it is worth while to consider whether a creed "answers" or not. He wishes to confound the whole school of those who think that a faith is to be tested by the inward experience of life. And so he sets himself to overwhelm Mr Hughes with ridicule, rioting in that kind of banter vulgarly described as "chaff," and bringing up against him the stock difficulties which can always be cast in the way of belief. And he does this in order to show Mr Hughes and his associates that they are "darkening counsel by words without knowledge."

But before they admit that they are finally extinguished by this battery of ridicule, Mr Hughes and his fellow-sufferers may appeal to the real nature of the question at issue. Supposing the question in its most essential form to be such as this, "Does God reveal himself to faith, or not? Can we hope to know anything about God, or not?"—the testimony of every man who is in earnest and who has appreciated for himself and others the gravity of the question must be worth something. Most of us surely would feel more helped by knowing the serious convictions of an honest mind than by seeing such convictions made game of. Just that part of the religious literature of all ages which has been most prized and has actually stirred the minds of men with the greatest power,—the utterance of what men have felt and inwardly proved,—is that which the reviewer denounces as futile.

This reviewer himself, as I have intimated, when he becomes most reverent, naturally invokes the same kind of personal experience. In the next month (Nov. 28th) the *Pall Mall Gazette* contained a review of the Archbishop of York's Lecture on the 'Limits of Philosophical Inquiry,' in the concluding part of which the writer threw his own views into the form of an allegory. It is almost too much to appropriate, but I find I cannot criticize it without transferring the whole of this interesting allegory to my pages.

"I dreamt that I was in the cabin of a large ship, which was filled with people divided into various groups listening to men who were explaining to them the beginning, the nature, and the end of their voyage, and the rules of navigation by which it was regulated. The different speakers did not agree. There was a general resemblance between their accounts, but there were also wide differences between them on which they insisted with extreme eagerness. All, however, seemed to think that to adhere with absolute confidence to the teaching of some one of them was an absolutely essential condition to every one who wished to complete the voyage prosperously. The cabin was handsomely furnished and brightly lighted, but there was something about it which filled me with depression and distrust. The various maps and charts to which the different speakers appealed were plain and systematic enough in parts, but in other parts they were exceedingly confused, obscure, and apparently contradictory, and when this was pointed out to the speakers they became enraged, and laid all the blame on the persons who pointed it out. Moreover, the general character of the prospects which they held out to us was horrible in the extreme. We were assured in every form of speech that what they had to tell was the best and most glorious news in the world; but when you put it all together the substance of it was that nearly every one of us must expect upon landing to be confined in a hideous dungeon, and there to be put to a cruel death by lingering torments. Some, we were told, were to be otherwise dealt with for reasons and upon principles which it was difficult to follow or apply, and all our teachers with one voice agreed in extolling with passionate raptures the glories of the country to which we were bound, and the wisdom, goodness, and mercy of its sovereign and its laws. Much saddened and somewhat confused with all this, I managed at last to make my way from the cabin to the deck, where I found myself enrolled, I could hardly tell how, amongst the crew who were working the ship. When I had time to look about me a little I observed several things which were strangely unlike the accounts given of the voyage in the cabin. Our ship was one on which the sun never shone. The voyage was made in the dark under a sky which was often cloudy, and where at best we got no other light than what came from the stars. We could never certainly tell whether we were in sight of land or not. In certain quarters of the sky there were indications of the shore, and here and there we thought we saw lights. Some of our crew declared that it was all nonsense; that there was no port and no shore at all, and that it was mere weakness and folly to think about them; that it was better to let the ship drive where she would than give ourselves so much trouble as we did to try to keep her to what was understood to be her course. The fact that there was such a course was the strangest thing about that strange vessel. Many theories there were about it, none of which were quite satisfactory. Yet it was a generally understood thing that, under all circumstances whatever, we were to steer due north, or as near thereto as we possibly could; and it was remarkable that the best and bravest and wisest of our crew would run incredible risks and undergo incredible dangers, often at the hands of companions who were dissatisfied with them, in order to keep the ship on that particular course. It was also very remarkable that when she was steered on any other it never turned out well in the end. Putting these things together, and connecting them with the fact that the ship obviously was a ship framed, equipped, and suited in every way to make a voyage, I could not help feeling that she was bound somewhere, and that she would find her port at last, although I doubted the wisdom of those who professed to know all about it. However this might be, I used to feel that I would try to do my duty, in the hope that it might turn out to have been a duty, and as

I stood on deck, with the fresh air blowing over me, the stars shining silently from the sky, and the ship leaning from the wind and riding over the seas with a motion full of freshness and vigour, I felt that there was something bracing in the very mystery with which I was surrounded, and that at all events ignorance honestly admitted and courageously faced and rough duty vigorously done was far better than the sham knowledge, the bitter quarrels, the sickly odours, and the glaring lamp-lights from which I had escaped."

The allegory does not seem to me in all points so transparent as the writer assumes it to be. I am not quite sure what the lamplight in the cabin means; but perhaps in this, and in more than this, there is an unintended echo of a remarkable passage in Isaiah (l. 10, 11): "Who is among you that feareth the Lord, that obeyeth the voice of his servant, that walketh in darkness, and hath no light? let him trust in the name of the Lord, and stay upon his God. Behold, all ye that kindle a fire, that compass yourselves about with sparks; walk in the light of your fire, and in the sparks that ye have kindled. This shall ye have of mine hand, ye shall lie down in sorrow." The resolution described in the allegory, I cannot but observe, is not far from what the prophet called "to trust in the name of the Lord, and to stay upon his

God." It is not quite obvious again how the people in the cabin are distinguished from those on deck, for it appears that amongst the crew also some thought one thing and some another; but probably the difference intended is between those who have opinions and those who work, or between speculation and matter of fact. Assuming that to be so, we observe that the crew, or the most sensible part of them, acted as if the ship were bound for a port. What was the ground of this action? There was "a general understanding" that a particular course was to be kept; "the best and bravest and wisest" of the crew were so satisfied in their own minds that they would encounter incredible risks and dangers to keep the ship on that course; and if the ship was steered on any other it never turned out well, or did not "answer." These things produce a "feeling" in the mind of the teller of the story. He "could not help feeling," he "used to feel," he "felt," that he would do his duty, "in the hope that it might turn out to have been a duty." There is singular deference on the part of the speaker to a mysterious kind of feeling. Everything is dark and uncertain to him; but he surrenders his persevering action, the dearest thing a man has to give, to be governed by the stronger convictions of the best and bravest and wisest, and by the experience of life. The ship looks as if it was meant to go somewhere; others tell him, and experience appears to support their belief, that it is to be steered on a particular course. Therefore he will do his part of the work as if it was his duty. We cannot withhold our respect from such a resolution; but what wins our respect is that the speaker does his duty in circumstances of such oppressive gloom, not that he despairs of receiving more encouragement. We should turn from him to inquire what the best and bravest and wisest who are so persuaded in their minds have to say about their hopes; and if we found that one of them was actually eager to explain his confidence so as to get others to share it, we should hardly meet his account of it with the question, Why can't you hold your tongue? It might turn out that the thoughts of these best and bravest and wisest, verified by their experience in working the ship, were worth putting side by side with the accounts, having a general resemblance to one another, of the speakers in the cabin. After all, there might be sunshine by times for those who knew where and how to look for it.

Remembering, however, the article on Mr Hughes, and other aggressive criticisms, I cannot help suggesting that the allegory needs a supplement, to some such effect as the following:

"Nevertheless I had a feeling as though it might be right for me to descend from time to time into the cabin, and to tell the people there what I thought of them. This was unfortunately a rough piece of duty, but finding it in me to do it vigorously and with enjoyment, I spent a considerable part of my time in the cabin, explaining to the various disputants all round the weaknesses I thought I could detect in their systems. On one of my visits to the cabin for this purpose, I observed a knot of persons who had offended the rest by declining to believe that the end of the voyage must necessarily be so gloomy as the majority expected it to be. These persons were endeavouring to dwell upon that general resemblance which I have mentioned above, in the hope of promoting unity; and they urged their fellow-passengers to look steadily to such indications as came to them from sky and water whilst they were working the vessel, and to compare these with the common statement in which the cabin-passengers agreed, instead of wrangling down in the cabin. It did not appear that this advice was receiving much attention, so I thought it might be practicable to silence this particular set. I noticed one of them, a cheery seaman, who made it his business to persuade people to come up on to the deck and help to work the ship, and who tried to put hope and heart into them by telling them in a very friendly way about his own feelings and experiences. No one could be angry with his kindly efforts, but I did not myself care much about his feelings or experiences, so I told him in a loud and rough voice, but with a good-humoured smile, that his talk was that of a canting humbug, and that it did not in the least matter to anybody what he had felt or observed, and that—unless indeed he could assure us that we were adrift without guidance on a sunless sea—he had better hold his tongue. I proceeded to banter him in a style which raised great laughter against him, and having done this I went on deck again much refreshed."

Although it is not, as I have said, the obvious moral of the allegory, yet the doctrine the writer desires to preach is chiefly this, that in the things by which our lives are governed certainty is unattainable, and the best knowledge no more than a supposition. And the strongest argument he adduces is an *argumentum ad verecundiam*. 'If the truth of what you are sure of were so evident, would not all men acknowledge it? But you know, or may know, that there are serious men, good men, who think your creed not only not certainly true, but even the reverse of true.' This difficulty has always existed, and the Gospel has won its conquests in the face of it. But from various causes the discouragement arising from it at the present time is greater than usual. We must recognize the force of the argument,—it ought to succeed in making us modest and respectful in all assertions of our faith. But the fact that there are men in earnest who do not believe in the Gospel, nor in a God who guides men's destinies and hears their prayers,—this and the many perplexities of which all thinking persons are conscious do not destroy the fact that many Christians have believed and still believe that the love of God revealed in Christ is one of the most certain things in the universe. Nor do all those difficulties necessarily make such confident assurance irrational. They must first make our hypothesis an absurd one. This is, that God reveals himself to faith. This has been the Christian hypothesis from the day when Jesus of Nazareth first proclaimed the kingdom of his Father. No wise Christian ever pretended that the Gospel could be demonstrated like the elements of geometry. The perpetual warning has been, Except ye be converted, and become as little children, ye cannot see, ye cannot enter into, the kingdom of heaven. All the mysticism and superstition and delusion that have cloaked themselves with this law cannot take away its authority as a primary condition of the faith of Christendom. If it is a true law, then assurance will naturally grow with spiritual insight. And before you can pronounce the assurance to be a delusion, you must shew that this law, not an afterthought but promulgated from the first, has no ground in reality.

And when we are thus bidden to be sure that we cannot be sure about our faith and our hope, another fact of great importance, depending upon the connexion between belief and life, forces itself upon our observation. When you have said 'This or that is highly probable,' if this or that be a relation involving life and action, the probability will of itself grow into certainty. Imagine a young man at the threshhold of his manhood to be satisfied that the existence and providence of God are highly probable suppositions. This hypothesis is such a one as to affect his whole being to the inmost secrets of his consciousness. God claims his trust, his love, his self-devotion. He goes on therefore to make his entire life an offering to God. Good and evil become to him inextricably associated with his conception of God. Sin, shame, self-approval, are rooted in the same belief. Imagine further that whilst he thus gives his affections to God, the hypothesis from which he starts is justified by all his inward experience. He has children, who must be taught something. He has a life in public, intercourse with his fellow-men, which must have one character or another. In his home, in society, he acts upon the hypothesis which commends itself to him more and more. He makes God's will the avowed rule of his life, he adores and loves God, he regularly prays to God. Is it an exaggeration to say that God will become to such a one the most certain reality in the universe? Life puts this constraint upon a man. He cannot always hesitate so much as he would like to do. No doubt this pressure is often trying to the conscience; no doubt it is an influence of which we ought to beware. We are in serious danger of being tempted to profess simply what it is expedient to profess. But this fact, that action is necessary and that it must spring from some assumption, agrees singularly well with the hypothesis that men individually and mankind in general are under a spiritual discipline, and are intended to learn as they go on.

It is a critical point in standing against such formidable assaults as those of the *Pall Mall Gazette* that we should take the right ground for resistance. But apart from attack and defence, it is of the highest importance for our own faith and life as Christians that we should stand where we are strongest or where God intends us to stand.

Let us be warned that the primary consideration, the question of questions, is whether we are under a Divine discipline or not. Is there a God, the Father of our spirits, dealing with us on the understanding that we are his children and so as to make us his true spiritual children? What are called *dogmas* assume their proper character when they are referred to this question. When they are separated from it, the assailant of dogmas gains an advantage, the Christian suffers loss, not only as against an opponent but for himself. It would be the removing of a stumblingblock if this misleading word dogma could be got rid of altogether. But let me illustrate by one or two examples from the *Pall Mall Gazette* the way in which a false issue may be taken about dogmas. Not long since it occurred to Mr Bright to say something favourable of the disposition of people in general. It did not seem a very original or hazardous observation; but the keen eye of our critic saw a use to be made of it. This is one symptom, he remarked, of the downfall of theology. The dogma of universal depravity is the cornerstone of all dogmatic theology, Catholic and Protestant; express any opinion to the effect that most persons mean well, and the whole edifice of theology comes tumbling about your ears. If so, I should say, let it fall. In one of the sermons of this volume I have endeavoured to explain the right sense and application of the Christian doctrine about human sinfulness. Here I will only remark that when the supposed edifice of dogma built up on the foundation of universal depravity has fallen into ruins, there remains simply untouched the Gospel of a living God who has reconciled mankind to himself and who seeks to make his children wholly pure and good. Again, in the article on the Archbishop of York's Lecture, the subject of self-sacrifice occurs. The writer maintains that absolute self-sacrifice is impossible in the Christian scheme. It is flatly inconsistent with a belief in future rewards. But how does he prove this? By assuming that self-sacrifice means self-injury. But in Scriptural and Christian language sacrifice does not mean injury or destruction, but offering. Sacrifice always implies a God to whom the offering is made. In the true sense of the word, there is no limit to the absoluteness of Christian self-sacrifice. The more thoroughly God is believed in as a just Father who rewards and punishes according to right, the more possible and reasonable does it become for a Christian to offer himself—to sacrifice himself—in absolute devotion to God. A third example may be found in what is a very favourite topic with the *Pall Mall Gazette*, the supposed Divine commission of the clergy. The clergy, it is never tired of insisting, have no supernatural functions. They are an educated class, whose opinions have value in proportion to their information. The most salutary of reforms would be to abolish the Ordination services. But *suppose*, I must repeat once more, that there is a God in heaven desiring that men should be reconciled to himself; then the fact that there is a class or order of men actually existing whose professed function it is to bear witness of the reconciliation which God has laid as the foundation of man's life cannot be thought of as unconnected with that other supposed fact. The supposition is to our minds strongly verified by the existence of such an order. The Gospel and the Ministry mutually commend each other. It would be a strange thing that for nearly two thousand years there should have been a succession of men accepting it as their office to declare solemnly in God's name that he had made peace between himself and mankind if this declaration had been a pure fiction. It would be inconceivable also that there should be a purpose of reconciliation in the mind of God and no utterance provided for this purpose. Those therefore who accept the simplest allegation of Christianity will inevitably believe also in some kind of Divine Commission for those whose calling it is to speak for God to men and to speak for men to God. To argue about the Divine Commission of the ministry of reconciliation as if it could mean nothing but some quackish miraculous powers deposited in the individual priest is surely to "darken counsel by words without knowledge."

In the true sphere of our faith the Gospel and the Church, as I have said, meet and sustain each other. The *Pall Mall Gazette* theology gives us a scheme of certain elementary propositions which may be considered probable,—as that God exists, that men are immortal, that virtue will be rewarded and vice punished,—and affirms that all the articles which constitute any "form of systematic theology," as they hang upon those first propositions, become less and less probable in a geometrical ratio. This statement of the case appears to me singularly unreal and unhistorical. That which Christians would substitute for it, to be tested by the proper criteria, would be something to this effect. Jesus Christ, by his actual life and by the witness of him which the Christian Church has carried on from age to age, has led Christendom to the Father. We in this day inherit a great tradition. The Church of our time and the Christian books of the age in which Christ lived tell us of a wonderful revelation of God. But this tradition must fail, as by its own profession it ought to fail, unless it is supported by the experience of the present, that is, by our own internal lives and by the common life of mankind. The Christian tradition gives us a certain account of God. We have considerable reason to accept the tradition as having a unique authority; we have considerable reason to accept, as good and true in itself, the account thus brought down to us of God. The tradition is supported by unrivalled historical evidence; its theology commends itself to us as meeting our needs and helping our progress. The agreement between the two contains the real force of the proof which sustains our faith. The Son is the way to the Father: we ascend by that way. The Father draws us to the Son: we yield to this attraction. We find the explanation of the twofold influence, where we find the light of the spiritual world and the object of our humble trust, in the unity of the Father and the Son.

I.

THE KINGDOM OF CHRIST AND THE CHURCH.

EPHESIANS I. 22.—"God gave him to be the head over all things to the Church."

THE Kingdom of Christ, or the coming of Christ to reign, is the general subject which the season of Advent suggests to us. I propose that we should consider this kingdom under three aspects,—as it is in relation to the Church, to the individual, and to the world. Our first inquiry will have reference to the Church. How does the acknowledgment of the Kingdom of Christ teach us to think of the Church of Christ?

The Church is an institution or creation which it is notoriously very difficult to define. *What is the Church?* Ask this question anywhere, and a score of answers will be given by those who are ready at defining, whilst those who are sensitive to difficulties will probably feel constrained to remain silent.

We speak of *the Church of Christ*, of *the Holy Catholic Church*. But when we look abroad upon the world, we see not a Church, but Churches. It is useless to disguise from ourselves those differences and disagreements with which Christians are taunted by unbelievers. Earnest Christians deplore them, and in deploring confess them. In this country there is our own Church, professing to be a national branch of the Church universal, holding the chief place. But on all sides of it there are bodies which call themselves Christian, standing aloof from its communion. The Roman Catholic Church is represented here; even the Greek Church has its congregations; whilst of non-Episcopalian sects, from the large and respectable societies of the Methodists, the Independents, and the Baptists, down to the smallest and most astonishing confessions, there are more denominations than can well be numbered. Each of these bodies, as a matter of course, regards itself as the most perfect and satisfactory Christian Church; but each of them is troubled what to say about the rest. I do not think there is more than one religious body which professes to be itself exclusively the Church of Christ. The Church of Rome, which in this country is numerically weak, elsewhere is the most imposing Church in Christendom. It carries on the tradition of the time when the Church was undivided. It still affirms, I believe, that there is no part of the real Church of Christ outside the Papal Communion,—that the Church of Rome is the Church Catholic, and the Church Catholic is the Church of Rome. But what can this doctrine mean, however loyally it may be professed with the lips, to an intelligent Christian-minded Roman Catholic who contemplates the vast Greek Church and the Church of England, not to speak of those whom we call Dissenters? Practically, such a Roman Catholic would acknowledge you and me as his fellow-Christians; and if he says that we do not belong to the Church of Christ, we are sure it must be in some not very hearty or natural sense.

Everywhere in Christendom, therefore, there is this difficulty of determining what the Church is. If we try to justify the open separation of Christians by dwelling upon the greatness and gravity of the differences of belief which make it impossible for them to worship together, how, we cannot help asking, can such a collection of communions excommunicating one another be called the Holy Catholic Church? If we try to make the most of the faith held by Christians in common and to treat their differences lightly, what is to be thought of the spirit animating these bodies, which holding, as we would fain believe, a common creed, find it impossible to worship as one communion? Where, under either supposition, is the Church of Christ?

There is a partial escape out of the difficulty, offered by the theory that there is an invisible Church, as well as a visible Church, of Christ,— the invisible consisting of persons in every communion who have the true faith in Christ and the true love of God, of which only God can be the

Judge, and the visible, which is of comparatively little consequence, and may therefore be held to include all who make any claim to belong to it. This doctrine has satisfied the religious needs of the greater number of pious Christians in this country, and has enabled them to live in Christian charity with their neighbours of different communions,—a service for which it deserves cordial respect. But it is an objection of some weight to this doctrine, that there is scarcely a hint of it in the New Testament, where all that is said of the Church of Christ evidently refers to the visible Church of baptized persons. And it has an inevitable tendency to create a kind of visible-invisible Church, of persons drawn together by the religious fashions of the day, and limited by tests which are imposed without any responsibility; and so a new kind of excommunication begins. Through this tendency the doctrine of an invisible Church of the truly religious persons in all visible Churches has already become discredited; and in many minds where it retains a traditional place it no longer serves the purpose of a genuine belief.

If there is a more excellent way to be shewn to you, that way, I believe, is to be found in looking to Christ as the Head of the Church, and seeing the unity of the Church in him only. This way, if it is one in which it is possible really to walk, is certainly the Scriptural way. The Church, in the New Testament, (and that is mainly in St Paul, who is the great expositor of the New Testament doctrine of the Church,) is *the body of Christ.* He is the head, men are the limbs. Or again, Christ is the foundation-stone or the corner-stone, the Church is built up of stones added to him. Or, as Christ himself said, he is the vine, his disciples are the branches. Or, Christ is the ruler of a commonwealth, which is the Church, of which Christians are citizens.

These Scriptural phrases are easy to quote,—some will think, too easy. The difficulty lies in connecting them with what we see to be the actual state of things. I have admitted that we see the Christianity of the world at the present moment distributed amongst an indefinite number of religious societies, holding all sorts of opinions, some of them violently antagonistic to each other. When we glance over modern Christendom, does it seem to be of any use to speak of the Church of Christ as a body of which Christ is the head, and his disciples the limbs? There is a visible and perfect unity in a healthy body: do the religious societies of Christendom exhibit any striking appearance of unity?

Now I would first observe that, if the idea of the Church as a body is not perfectly realized in the distracted Churches of our own day, neither was it so realized in St Paul's day. There is a difference in degree, no doubt. The Church of the Apostolic age had much more apparent, much more real, unity than modern Christendom. Many of the modern causes and features of disunion were then absent. But the members of the Churches to which the Epistles were written were too far from being spiritually organized into a perfect unity of subordination to Christ and agreement with one another to allow of that image of the body, or the other of a temple, being an exact representation of their state. Remember for our present purpose, what for other reasons it is often necessary to insist upon, that the Church of the first age was not composed of ideally perfect members. Theological controversies, personal jealousies, irregularities, shameful sins, darken all the records of that society which had for its immediate instructors and rulers the companions of Jesus Christ. That was no undivided body, to which St Paul addressed the reproach, "Ye are yet carnal: for whereas there is among you envying, and strife, and divisions, are ye not carnal, and walk as men?" I take it therefore as certain that St Paul was not merely describing the condition of things which he beheld in the Church around him, when he dwelt on the natural harmonies of the body, the limbs divinely tempered together, all with various functions inspired by one life and serving one will. That account of the full-grown Man, according to which "from Christ, who is the head, all the body, fitly framed together and compacted by means of every joint of the whole supply, according to the working in its measure of each several part, effects the growth of the body to the building up of itself in love," did not correspond precisely to the actual state of the Church as it then was at Ephesus, or at Corinth, or at Rome.

But St Paul would have said, 'That is what the Church, as the Church of Christ, *properly is*. I know that the Christian community at Corinth, or that at Ephesus, does not answer in its actual condition to such an account; but that is because these communities are not perfect as branches of the Church of Christ. The true character of the Church is striving, under Divine grace, to realize itself amongst them in spite of all their divisions and sins; that amongst foolish and sinful men it has prevailed and manifested itself as it has done, however imperfectly that may be, is a triumph of Divine grace.'

What I thus suppose St Paul to have said, we may even now say. We may take that image, of the Church as a body of which Christ is the head, exactly as St Paul left it to us, and may say, The Church of Christ is realized amongst all these Christians, just so far as they fulfil the conditions of that image. The Church of Christ is not the Roman Church, or the Greek Church, or the Anglican, or Protestant Christendom, nor is it the mere aggregation of all these bodies: it is the spiritual body which is partially realized in each of these. If we were able to form a true and vivid conception of what the perfect Church of Christ would be in modern times,—and we might approach to such a conception,—if we could bring before our minds an image of all men and all societies discharging those functions which the Divine Creator and Ruler assigns to them in perfect subordination to the Divine Will and therefore in perfect mutual service and harmony, we might place such an image by the side of every Christian Church and people, and we might say, The one Catholic Church of Christ is there, in that country, just so far as this image can be seen in their actual constitution and life: nothing prevents us from recognizing there the noble features, the beneficent energy, of the perfect Church, except the ignorance and perversity of men.

I think that this conception of the Church,—this way of understanding what the one Church truly is,—will be found to bear using. It enables us to do justice, in proportion to our knowledge, to every Church. We shall not feel compelled to make out that one Church is peculiarly guaranteed in any manner or degree as the true Church, or as a branch of the true Church. We shall not depend, with many and painful misgivings, upon doctrinal formularies or Apostolical institutions as separating off a safe fold from the unrecognized Christendom around. We shall judge ourselves as we shall judge others. And we shall see a hope, a real and the best hope, of a true unity to come out of present divisions, in the endeavour of every man and of every society to be spiritually true to the Divine ideal, and so to realize a portion of the one perfect Church.

A fear may be felt that in thus thinking of the Church as a Divine ideal partially realized wherever there is Christian faith and life, we are leaving fact and taking refuge in imagination. The Holy Catholic Church, it might be apprehended, becomes nothing more than a theory of some men's minds as to what a Church ought to be.

In reply to such an apprehension I would make two observations.

1. That ought not to be called a mere imagination or theory, which we recognize as a living and working reality. This Church of Christ, of which I speak, does not depend upon our notions of what is right; it is actually alive amongst ourselves, so far as we are loyal to Christ. All true relations amongst us, so far as they are not marred by our unfaithfulness; all spiritual life, so far as we do not quench it by our worldliness,—are the constitution and the activity of that one body of which Christ is the head. We see a human body which is deformed and sickly; we say that the true human form is in that case distorted or mutilated, that the true human health is weakened and corrupted; and no one supposes that the normal human form or the due human health is a mere fiction; we see them both, interfered with but not destroyed, in the deformed and sickly body. So we may justly and usefully speak of the one Church of Christ as established and living all over the earth. It only needs growth, redemption, perfection, to reveal itself everywhere in all its beauty.

2. The second observation is this. We shall guard ourselves from unreality in this contempla-

tion of an ideal Church by looking steadfastly to Christ and acknowledging him as the living Head. "Holding the Head," this St Paul knew to be the great security. There is no need for any of us to struggle with a dull imagination, and to try to call up an ideal before our minds, and to be continually in fear lest we should lose it,—if only we can keep ourselves alive to the presence of Christ the Head. Christ, rightly apprehended, carries the Church with him. To know Christ after the flesh is to know him as an isolated person, whether we confess him to be Divine or not; to know men after the flesh is to know them as connected by none but fleshly ties. To know Christ and men after the Spirit, is to know them as bound together— Christ to them, and they to Christ, in a glorious fellowship and order. To the spiritual eye, Christ is evermore the Head of a redeemed humanity. He is not to be thought of, except as ordering and giving life to "the Church which is his body."

To know Christ therefore as actually reigning through and by means of the bonds and relations which unite spiritual men, and as exercising his power towards the end of bringing men into a true spiritual fellowship,—this is the best way to know what the Church means.

We may see advantages in the definition of truth; we may be led to regard dogmatic formularies as useful and indispensable. But if we are knowing the Church through the living royalty of a Head who cannot be without members and who claims believing men as his members, we shall not be able to think of any part of the Church as having its genuine life or support in its articles of faith. The Church or congregation of fallible sinful men will have its truth and life in conforming to the conditions of the ideal Church,—that is, in being brought near to God in the Spirit through Christ. Every Church will be rightly guided towards perfection and the desired unity by spiritual allegiance to Christ. Thus it will be taught to put on what is good, to put off what is evil; to adopt whatever will effectually bring mankind into the true fellowship, to discard whatever is a cause of disunion and isolation.

If there are any amongst you, who are disposed to see something like perfection in our own Church, who rejoice in it as a national Church, and yet rejoice also that it cherishes an hereditary and traditional connection with the Christian Church of the older centuries, who believe that it has sought, not unsuccessfully, to preserve a spiritual theology, who revere it as being—to use a common eulogy—Evangelical in doctrine and Apostolical in order: I, for one, sympathize too much with these feelings to find any fault with them. But I may ask you not to be too satisfied or too confident. Let us keep our eyes not upon what seem the faults or defects of our neighbours, but upon the advancing perfection of the ideal Church; let us strive to be brought nearer and nearer to the Divine harmony and health of the body of Christ. Let us remind ourselves, also, to hold fast and value these Anglican principles of ours, not as instruments of separation from other communions, but as bonds uniting us to Christ and therefore also constraining us to cherish sympathy with all other men. If our Church is a better Church than others, let us shew it by our humility and sense of unworthiness, by our longing for improvement of every kind, by the courage of our sympathy with everything that is godly and Christlike in the world.

The language of the New Testament bids us think of Christ as having come to reign before the close of the Apostolic age. If the thought of the universal Church is to us a great conception, filling our minds and feeding our imaginations, we cannot but believe that that was an important coming of Christ to reign, when the local centre of the Divine Covenant and worship, the Holy City and Temple, was removed out of the way, and Christ was revealed to the conscience and understanding of his followers as the invisible Head and Ruler of the Church of all mankind. The movement by which the universal Church was fairly launched upon the world and constrained to know its Head as only in heaven, was a great Advent of Christ.

But the more we dwell upon that Advent, and the more we interest ourselves in the present condition of the Church of Christ,—the more are we driven and encouraged to look also to the future. The most earnest and active members of the Church of Christ have always been sustained by hopes of a coming redemption. We can see now that their definite anticipations have generally been moulded by their merely human imagination or fancy, and any empty-hearted critic can laugh at their prophecies. But we may also see, if we will, that the substance of their various expectations was simply the coming of Christ in his glory. They longed for the time when through judgments and through the outpouring of the Spirit Christ should be known and confessed as the Head of his Church, and the Church should be seen victoriously fulfilling its Divine destiny. Such a hope can never die out from the hearts of Christians till all Christian faith is itself extinct. A Christian cannot live in the present only. His present necessarily rests upon the past, and leads him back to the past; and as he feeds by faith upon what the Father formerly did in sending his Son and exalting him to his own right hand and giving him to be the Head over all things to the Church, his expectations of what must be the final issue of such Divine acts become boundless in their ambition. If God has given a kingdom to his Son, he could not mean that he should be for ever disobeyed and thwarted. If there is a true Church of Christ, it cannot be the will of the Eternal that it should remain disguised, and unrecognized, and buried under human ignorance and corruptions as it is at present. No, we must hope for better things; we must hope for a full redemption to come; and the glory of the future to the Christian can only be the coming of his Lord to reign unveiled in his kingdom.

II.

THE KINGDOM OF CHRIST AND THE CHRISTIAN.

COLOSSIANS I. 13.—"Who hath delivered us from the power of darkness, and hath translated us into the kingdom of his dear Son."

IN this sermon we are to consider how the coming of Christ to reign may be regarded as affecting *the individual man*. In the last we inquired how, when we confess Christ as King, we are led to think of *the Church*. We now remember that the Church is made up of individuals, each with a distinct spiritual life; and we ask, How is any one of us, as an individual, concerned with the coming and kingdom of Christ? What difference does it make to one or another, as he lives his personal life, that Christ has come and is coming?

There is a saying which is true in a sense, but which is also, as it is often used and understood, very untrue, that religion is a purely personal matter between God and a man's own soul. It is quite true that ultimately every man is responsible to God only, and that men are very incompetent judges and critics of a brother's faith. It is well that we should all learn to say, "With me it is a very small thing that I should be judged of you or of man's judgment...he that judgeth me is the Lord." But if that saying is meant or understood to imply that religion isolates a man from his fellow-men,—that in matters of religion, as distinct from those of secular life, a man stands alone by himself,—there may possibly be some kinds of religion with reference to which it may be true, but it is signally untrue of any which can properly be called Christian. It belongs essentially to the Christian religion to deal with individuals from first to last as *not* standing alone in their relations to God. It assumes that a man is, and may know himself to be, most closely related to other men, and it seeks to cherish all the sentiments and convictions which belong to corporate life.

And yet it is a fact, which no religion denies or could induce us to forget, that each of us has his distinct personal life. In every man there is the mystery of the individual consciousness, carrying with it a personal responsibility,—of a will choosing its own objects and working out its own issues, —of secrets which we do not share with our fellow-men,—of a private susceptibility to joy and sorrow which is separately touched by the common outward influences. In those relations to God and to our fellow-men which Christian faith recognizes, each man is a unit, though he does not stand alone. It is a question of the deepest interest, therefore, how we, as distinct individuals, stand affected by the great revelation of Christ ruling in his kingdom. The personal conscience and personal will are not swallowed up by the corporate life of the Christian Church. It is one of the glories of the Christian scheme of human life, that by learning how he is bound to God and his fellow-men a man also learns most truly and thoroughly what he is for himself.

When we turn our thoughts backwards upon ourselves, the little fragment of each man's personal existence, bounded by his life and death, shut in by the insurmountable barriers of circumstance, is apt to seem appallingly insignificant. Take for example that old illustration,—"For what is your life? It is even a vapour, that appeareth for a little time, and then vanisheth away." Like a puff of vapour, so frail, ineffectual, and transitory,—is a man's life no more than that? What is it makes us ask such a question,—what is it that causes our life, such as it is, to make this impression of insignificance upon our minds? It is no doubt the *contrast* between the indefinite largeness of our thoughts and interests and the smallness of one man's life, the little space occupied by one life as compared with that vastness of the universe which we can more or less comprehend with the imagination. We have power to think of the indefinite past, of the indefinite future, of the breadth and the length of human history, of the indefinite greatness of the Divine purposes. What is my little bit of a life in this world of thought? Less than a drop in the ocean.

We cannot destroy this fact of the proportion between one human life and the vast imagined world. The fact will remain. But we may learn to accept it without bitterness or cynicism, if we can perceive that our individual existence is justified and exalted, and that we in reality *find ourselves*, by sharing intelligently to the utmost of our spiritual power in the great Divine movements, and by throwing ourselves heartily and thankfully into the work of the Divine will. We are not compelled to alternate between boundless aspirations and the despair of self-contempt. All the scornful disparagements of human strength and life will not touch a soul that is laid hold of and strengthened by the living purposes of God. The Word of God, coming into men, makes them from men into gods.

Let us place ourselves, as individuals, in the presence of Christ ruling in his Kingdom. What are the impressions which form themselves in our minds? They will be such as these.

1. If Christ is a King, we, so far as we are Christ's, belong to a Kingdom. There is the King ruling in heaven; we are his subjects. Each man, John or James or Paul, is not a mere accident; he is not a thing of flesh and blood; he is not a waif or stray cast upon this visible stage of pleasures and pains. He belongs to a commonwealth, he is a King's subject.

We may let our thoughts busy themselves upon the various conditions which the idea of a Kingdom seems to imply, and may ask how we find ourselves circumstanced in this Kingdom of Christ. The centre and principal reality is the King; and he is the Son of God, the Lord Jesus Christ. There must be laws of the Kingdom, and those laws will be the various manifestations of the Divine mind. Has the Kingdom a history? Has it enemies? Are there officers, are there ranks, in it? Have we fellow-citizens? Have we a birthright and privileges? Do we look for promotion and reward? To these and similar questions we may obtain answers more or less definite and certain. And so we shall get to understand better what we are and why we have come into the world and what we have to do. The main point of all is that we try to think rightly, if we can, of the King, in whom the Kingdom has all its form and life.

2. The commonwealth of which Christ is the head, we cannot help observing, includes past and future generations, as well as the present. Each individual of the present age is linked, in this Kingdom, to innumerable fellow-subjects who have gone before, and to a vaster multitude who are to follow after. The King of all lives in the unseen world; and we cannot think of him as having none but visible subjects. The first founders of the commonwealth are to us still fellow-subjects. We see others of our own time passing into the invisible world without any rupture of their relations with the King or with their predecessors in the commonwealth. We look forward to treading in the same path, and leaving others to follow us. We learn to

live not only in the present but also in the past and the future. This faculty, this prerogative of humanity, grows and is strengthened with our growth as believers in Christ and his Kingdom.

3. And so we learn to feel that our most important relations are *spiritual*. Through the eye and the ear and the touch,—through all the physical senses,—I am manifestly related to outward things. I have that in me which craves pleasure; I have that in me which shrinks from pain. We see around us creatures which seem to be governed solely by such a desire of physical pleasure and such an avoidance of physical pain. The brute beasts are moved by their bodily instincts. So are we. But is that all, with us? Are we in the same rank with the brute beasts? The man who confesses Christ as King feels himself to be in another world from that of the bodily senses and pleasures and pains. He has to do with powers which eye cannot see and hand cannot handle. He must live as one to whom invisible things are real; and if they are *real* to him, these invisible powers are also transcendant and sovereign. No man can acknowledge Christ as Lord, and with any rational consistency make the concerns of the daily outward life of more importance to him than those which bind him to Christ. Under the fostering influence of this dominant spiritual relation—the bond between the man and his Lord,—all spiritual ties and affections are able to grow and flourish. The Christian's life becomes essentially a spiritual one.

His relations with visible persons and things are transfigured. As he looks at them, the outward phenomena disappear in a heavenly glory. The bonds of parent and child, of husband and wife, of mutual dependence and service, are things of the unseen world, fraught with spiritual significance. Whether a man eats or drinks or whatever he does, he sees that it is possible to do all to the glory of God. All physical enjoyment may be made to minister to the great spiritual joy of thankfulness. Physical privation and pain may be made another road to the same goal, when a man needs to be taught sharply not to look downwards but to look upwards. The thankfulness taught by pain is in the end deeper and richer than that prompted by pleasure. And thus through knowing Christ after the Spirit, the Christian learns to know no man, and even no thing, only after the flesh.

To be truly human in the personal life is—to *live by spiritual relations;* and there has been no such way of realizing spiritual relations as that of contemplating Christ in his kingdom. The most remarkable attainment of spiritual sight and consciousness of which we have any knowledge was in the case of the disciples of Christ after his death. Whilst he was with them in the flesh, their conceptions were persistently carnal. Their spiritual apprehensions were weak and rare. But when he had gone to his Father's house, he prepared room for them, and came again and received them to himself, so that where he was, there they were also.

They learnt to live in fellowship and as it were companionship with their Master, whom they saw at the Father's right hand. They too became thus inmates of the Father's house, subjects and citizens of a heavenly commonwealth. And a similar result must always follow a similar faith. Let a Christian know Christ in his Kingdom with anything like clearness and steadiness, and it is impossible that he should not live in the Spirit. He will see with the mind where the eye can see nothing; that which his eye sees will be a medium revealing to him the unseen.

4. And, to speak more definitely of the ruling law of the spiritual life, if we contemplate Christ as King, we shall feel that we owe him a *personal allegiance*.

When he was on earth amongst disciples, leading and teaching and comforting them, he called himself the true Shepherd. And he said, "My sheep hear my voice, and I know them, and they follow me." He had at that time followers who *did* recognize him as their spiritual Master, and listened for his directions, and loyally obeyed them. When he went to his Father, these followers continued to follow him. They remembered the life he had led, going in and out amongst them, and they set themselves to walk in his steps. But this was not the only method of their following. They believed that they could still hear his voice. They believed that he was near them in the Spirit, speaking to them in many ways, telling what he desired, shewing them the ways in which he would have them walk. They were liable to mistake other suggestions for his instructions, but their security from error was found in watchful loyalty to the great principles of his character, righteousness and love.

With us, brethren, it is a great thing, and certainly a main part of our allegiance, that we should consider the example of the Lord Jesus as the Gospels have enabled us to become acquainted with it, and bear in mind that, as Christians, we also ought to walk even as he walked. The most obvious and universal way of attaining any knowledge of Christ at all is through what is communicated to us, directly or indirectly, by Holy Scripture. But when we have come to know him, we do not fully discharge our allegiance to him by trying to copy the example of which we find the traces in that volume. The higher and truer kind of following is to hear his voice still speaking to us and to answer to his summons. It is impossible, indeed, to urge obedience to the living voice of our Master at the present time without remembering how difficult it is found by many who would gladly hear that voice to make sure that it is now speaking in tones that we can recognize. The difficulty is a genuine one, and no remarks in a sermon can do much to remove it. But I may ask Christians to be more careful to connect together the dominion of Christ and those directions, however they may come, by which men are practically led in the ways of righteousness and peace. All such guidance must really come from him who rules in heaven. And we may trust the testimony of the loyal followers of Christ, that if we confess his sovereignty in our inmost hearts, and honestly seek to be guided by him who is the uttered Righteousness and Love, we shall find our desire met, our prayers answered. Only let us not limit the variety of the ways which he uses, nor think channels which we call *secular* unworthy of the Lord of heaven and earth. You will easily acknowledge that in proportion as we can behold Christ in his Kingdom, we shall believe in the unlimited range of his authority, and shall feel bound to surrender ourselves in all things to his guidance.

The question sometimes comes before us, as a practical and important one, Are we to be guided by old precedents or by the indications of new circumstances? Shall we go by the rules which old experience has laid down, or shall we take into consideration the facts of life and history which have grown up since those rules were given? In such cases trust in a living Guide, loyalty to a living Ruler, will have power to sway our judgment. Those who believe in a Kingdom of Christ making a history for itself out of the ages as they roll on will be prepared for new circumstances and will desire fresh light from heaven to shew how new things are to be dealt with.

5. Lastly, then, when we stand face to face with the Kingdom of Christ, we feel that it is our

privilege and duty, single shortlived human beings as we are, to interest ourselves in this progress of its dominion. Let it be true that we are insignificant and weak. But the Kingdom of Christ is great and powerful. We may forget ourselves, we may lose ourselves, in the great interests of the Divine Kingdom, and find a blessedness in doing so. My brethren, this would be the perfecting at the same time of God's universal government and of our individual destinies,—that we should give ourselves intelligently and willingly to the accomplishment of the work of the Kingdom, and therein find ourselves entirely satisfied. I can hardly imagine any one doubting that such a scheme would be the perfect reconciliation of the universe and of the individual man, the perfect blending of the Divine purpose and of the movements of single lives. There can hardly be a lot better or more satisfying to a human soul, than to see with trust and hope the Fatherly mind of God drawing on the progress of his creation from the worse to the better, from the less perfect to the more perfect, from the material and carnal life to the spiritual and heavenly, from struggles for existence to the contented harmony of fellow-work and mutual kindness,—to see enough for faith of that progress and to be called upon to work with it. · To a soul which thus sees and believes and hopes, what is it that its own sphere is narrow, that its own powers are small? There is no place in that soul for discontent or jealousy or self-worship; it is drawn out into reverence and activity and love.

Such a personal existence, I repeat, is offered to us by the revelation of the Kingdom of Christ. We are taught by the traditions of our faith that the Divine Kingdom entered as a universal kingdom into human history, that the Son of man took possession of his throne, at a given time,—namely, when the Covenant of a special people was finally superseded by the Covenant of humanity. The anticipations cherished by believers in this Kingdom as to its future glory and triumph have had the marks of eagerness and impatience upon them as well as those of hope and joy. This has always been the character of such anticipations; it would be so again, no doubt, if our faith were lively enough to give them new birth. If we were so earnest in pursuit of purity and peace, so intolerant of evil, as to cry, How long, O Lord, how long?— we should see again in the terrors and afflictions of our time the signs of an end of the world such as has not yet come to pass, of a consummation more final than any that has been. As it is, our faith is weak, our assurance takes no hold. We are almost afraid to think much of the Presence and Coming of Christ. We see that our fathers have been deceived; we are shy of becoming the victims of new delusions. Well, let us cry earnestly to heaven, Lord, increase both our faith and our light. And in the mean time let us feed our convictions and hopes upon the things that we can see. We see, I venture to say, such a progress of Christ's Kingdom as agrees with the methods of Divine action. We see a spreading of light slow, but real, over humanity, we see a higher standard of judgment establishing itself; we see modes of work, ends of endeavour, presenting themselves everywhere, with all new phases of life, to sincere believers in Christ. We hear the summons repeated, and coming home to each of us personally, You that are children of the day, cast away the works of darkness, and put on the armour of light. Christ is your Captain in the warfare in which you are engaged. He shews you the enemies you are to attack, he shews you where you may plant the standard of his Kingdom of light. There are follies and corruptions which the world admires or tolerates, which are nothing better than things of darkness, against which you are to protest, which it is your business as children of the light to reprove. There is sensual degradation out of which nothing but a new heart and a right spirit, given from above, can lift men. There are graces of reverence, of kindness, of purity, of happy industry, of mutual help, to be won for our homes and cities and villages by the earnest spiritual effort of faithful men and women. You see your calling, brethren; you are enlisted as soldiers in Christ's army, you may help forward the success of his Kingdom. Will you take this in faith for the work of your lives? Will you redeem, each man and each woman, your several days from their insignificance and barrenness and discontent, by consecrating them loyally to the service of him who has bought them?

III.

THE KINGDOM OF CHRIST AND THE WORLD.

1 Cor. x. 26.—"The earth is the Lord's, and the fulness thereof."

We have considered on recent Sundays how the confession of Christ as reigning and about to reign affects our view of *the Church*, and also how the destinies and duties of *the individual man* appear to us when seen in the light of the same confession. These are the relations which occur to us first:— Christ and the Church of Christ, Christ and the Christian. But we must not stop at these. We must go on to speak of Christ and *the world* together. We are urged forward by the necessary tendency of our inquiries, as well as by the pretensions of our faith, to ask, What is Christ to the world? How will the world appear to us, when regarded in its connection with Christ?

There is sometimes a danger of ambiguity and confusion when we use this term "the world;" but for our present purpose it does not need any careful defining. We mean by *the world* the whole body of mankind with their secular organizations,— all nations and kindreds and people and tongues, whether they belong to Christendom or not. That Christ is the Head of his Church, that the single Christian owes him allegiance, are obvious articles of our faith. But there are empires and kingdoms and republics as well as Churches; there are hundreds of millions of human beings who do not profess to acknowledge Christ. What has the Lordship of Christ to do with the kingdoms of this world and the various races of mankind?

One tempting answer is to say, "Nothing. The kingdom of Christ is spiritual, the world is secular. Christ and his servants seek to win souls; but they have nothing to do with the affairs of this world." This answer is supported by two well-known texts,—that is to say, by misinterpretations of them. Jesus said, "My kingdom is not of this world." That is, really, "My kingdom is not *from* this world." He did not say that his kingdom was not *over* this world, that it was not *in* this world; but that it was not derived, that it did not obtain its authority and strength, from this world. Again, Jesus said, "Render unto Cæsar the things that are Cæsar's, and to God the things that are God's." But he did not therefore say that Cæsar and God have separate dominions, and that where Cæsar rules God has no authority. Our Lord no doubt held what St Paul plainly taught, that it was right to render his dues to Cæsar, *because* Cæsar was ordained of God,—that we pay tribute to civil rulers, because they are God's ministers.

This theory of the natural separation of the

Divine and the secular provinces is the mere refuge of a narrow or an indolent mind. It will not bear one moment's sincere and thorough thought. In all the prophecies and aspirations of the New Testament relating to the coming of Christ's kingdom, we find the secular organizations of mankind claimed as subject to him. Thus St Paul says (Eph. i. 21) that when God raised up Christ from the dead, and set him at his own right hand in the heavenly world, he placed him "far above all principality and power and might and dominion and every name that is named, *not only in this world*, but also in that which is to come." In the book of Revelation the subject of the visions is the triumph of the kingdom of Christ over *the world*. These are its boasts,—" The kingdoms of this world are become the kingdoms of our Lord and of his Christ; and he shall reign for ever and ever." "I saw heaven opened, and behold, a white horse; and he that sat upon him was called Faithful and True, and in righteousness he doth judge and make war. His eyes were as a flame of fire, and on his head were many crowns...And he hath on his vesture and on his thigh a name written, King of kings and Lord of lords." Of the city which descended out of heaven from God it is said, "The nations of them which are saved shall walk in the light of it; and the kings of the earth do bring their glory and honour unto it." Such visions cannot but float before the mind of every sincere and earnest Christian. Confess Christ as your own Lord, confess him as the Lord of the Church, and it is impossible you should not claim for him all dominion in earth as well as in heaven. If you acknowledge him as ruling now, though we do not yet see all things put under his feet, (in the Church or in the soul of any man, any more than in the world,) how does the rule of Christ take effect in the present history of the world? In other words, what has God to do with the fortunes of nations, with the struggles of races? If we ascend to the top of a high mountain and survey all the kingdoms of the world and the glory of them, how do they place themselves in our mind with reference to the kingdom of God?

If I assume that it is *difficult* for us to think of governments and dynasties, of commerce and war, of races and languages, of all the social and political interests of mankind, as working out, whether through obedience or conflict, the purposes of the Kingdom of Christ, I do not imagine that any of you, brethren, will be inclined to question the difficulty. The habit of thought to which I refer is a different thing from that study which many have found fascinating as a mere exercise of ingenuity—the study of the fulfilment of prophecy. We have more and other things to interpret than what the frogs mean, and the little horn, and the drying up of Euphrates. We may reasonably confess our incompetence as interpreters. We need not consider ourselves bound as Christians to put a distinct meaning upon this event and upon that, as working out the Divine will. If we try to do so, we may expect to make many mistakes. But we must admit, whatever the admission may cost, that a Christian's faith is not securely grounded until he has the habitual feeling that a Divine hand is leading and controlling the nations, until he believes that, whether he can see it or not, all political and historical movements are working out the ends of the Kingdom of Christ. Our faith in Christ ought not to be divided from, but should coalesce with, our interest as citizens and as men.

It is as helping towards such a faith and consciousness that I offer the following observations.

1. First, God is slow and patient. We who think and learn and believe and interpret are single human beings, each but one out of the innumerable host of our fellow-men, each with the short life of a few years out of all time, each with a small sphere of existence out of all creation: and when we measure ourselves, as it were, in thought against the great developments which constitute history, we can scarcely fail to find ourselves continually *out of proportion* with them. We cannot easily adjust ourselves to the wide and gradual march of events. It is our human privilege and prerogative to speculate; and, as we speculate, we contract things within too narrow a compass. We try to trace things to their causes; and the causes we assign to them are apt to be too near, too limited and partial. We look for issues in the future from causes which we see to be in operation now; and

those issues are almost always brought too near, and made too definite and isolated. Always as we know more, things that were thought to be near are found to be more remote. Origins recede back further and further into the past, till they go out of our sight. Ends of the world move away in front of us faster than we approach them. This is the general experience of mankind as the stock of knowledge increases. We have learnt in some degree to be on our guard against the tendency to abridge and reduce the movements of the world to the proportions of individual existence. But every mind is liable over again to the same infirmity of nature. The sharp and vigorous conclusions concerning the ways of Providence which spring really from the deep roots of a faithful and earnest mind, and which therefore have more spiritual truth in them than many lazy generalizations, are likely to be at fault in this point of the proportion of time and space. St Paul, with his inspired wisdom, compares the intellectual conceptions of the best Christians to those notions of our childhood at which adult age smiles. "We know in part, and we prophesy in part. But when that which is perfect is come, then that which is in part shall be done away. When I was a child, I spake as a child, I understood as a child, I thought as a child; but when I became a man, I put away childish things." Now one step for the Christian in putting away childish things is to realize that God works more slowly and over a larger space than we had supposed. God "tarries," as devout men have always been led to see. We also have to learn patience from God's patience. We must not resent it, if the drama of Divine Providence turns out to be much vaster and more complicated than we had conceived it. Let us endeavour to see that we have not been baffled as to principles, as to spiritual realities, if measurements of time and space prove to have been incorrect. Let us desire that our thoughts may be expanded to take in the greatness of the Divine operations as God reveals them to us.

People who fancy that because primitive notions about the Coming of Christ and the end of the world have been corrected by experience therefore the primitive faith was only a delusion, are those who have an eye for the outward shell but can take no account of the inner spiritual reality. The faith of Christendom has to shed many shells and coatings of external and material conceptions as it grows and enlarges. We often have to learn anew the old lesson, that God's thoughts are not our thoughts, neither are our ways his ways. For as the heavens are higher than the earth, so are God's ways higher than our ways, and his thoughts than our thoughts.

2. Another reflection which will be useful to us in connecting our faith in Christ's Kingdom with the contemplation of the world is this,—that God works and reveals himself most properly in the victories of what we call *moral principles*, such as

righteousness, order, goodwill. What is called in one language the progress of civilization, is, in another language,—that of Christian faith,—called the advance of Christ's Kingdom.

We may well be sorry for those who can speak of nothing but civilization and equal justice, and who cannot see the living fountain of human order and happiness in the God who made himself known by the sending of his Son. But we must take care that we ourselves, who worship God through his Son Jesus Christ, do not separate him in our habitual thoughts from the righteousness and love which are the essence of his nature, the living characters of his Name.

You will remember that when the Hebrew prophets saw Jehovah reigning and judging, the signs in their eyes of the Divine Kingdom were always the righteousness, the peace, the order, the prosperity, which were established on the earth. Truth and goodness could come from no other than the Lord God. Where wrongs were righted, where the oppressor was laid low, where the poor and meek were comforted, where the wilderness was made to blossom, where joy and hope and energy were planted, there was the reign of the Lord manifested.

Let me recall some words I have already quoted from the great New Testament prophecy. When heaven was opened to the seer, he saw a white horse; "and he that sat upon him was called Faithful and True, and in righteousness he doth judge and make war......His Name is called *The*

Word of God. And the armies in heaven followed him upon white horses, clothed in fine linen, white and clean." It is evident that the seer of this vision recognized in all historical events by which oppression was punished, and justice and purity promoted, the direct action of him through whom God utters himself in the creation and in human history. The leader of the pure and righteous host is *The Word of God.* Where justice is done on earth, there is God speaking with his heavenly power; and where God speaks, there we recognize the presence of him in whom the Father spoke once and speaks for evermore, his Son Jesus Christ.

Would it not become less difficult for us, brethren, to see the Kingdom of Christ advancing, if we were accustomed to look for it in the moral action upon human affairs of him who is called Faithful and True, and whose Name is the Word of God? It is a danger besetting professedly religious persons, to think of the Kingdom of Christ exclusively in connection with religious organizations and creeds. I am not intending to disparage these instruments of Christ's Kingdom. But I think it important to point out to you, as I have done, that the very essence of the authority of Christ as manifested on earth is the assertion of justice and goodwill. This is what the Scriptures teach us. It sometimes happens, as no one can refuse to admit, that Christian men and Christian Churches offend against justice and love in the very name of religion.

And then the royal judgment of Christ can only be seen in the humiliation of the religious man or the Christian Church. In other cases, we may see a genuine zeal for righteousness and goodness and self-sacrifice in those who do not profess to be religious, whom we should not acknowledge as orthodox, or who are not even by name Christians. What are we to say then?—We may consider it one of the strange and puzzling anomalies in human things that the very Word of God should be speaking through those who have not learned to see God's glory in the face of Jesus Christ: but we must confess that it is the Word of God that speaks; and we ought to rejoice that, through whatever means, the Divine Word is asserting his dominion.

The great spiritual or moral principles by which the perfection of mankind is secured may serve for a meeting-point and reconciliation, in this way. Let us look at history and judge of events and politics always from the moral point of view. Let us look for the genuine *good* that there is in every thing. Let us do this on the one side. Then, on the other, let us accustom ourselves to think of the Divine Kingdom as working through the vindication and establishment of the Divine morality. Thus, secular history and the Kingdom of the Word of God will be brought to one focus in our minds. We shall see Christ wherever we see essential civilization.

3. A third consideration is this. The Coming of Christ is most often described in Scripture as

the Coming of *the Son of man.* Let us take this name as significant. Then whatever tends to the advance and union of *humanity* is a part of the glory of the Son of man. Now it is a generally admitted fact that the progress of history from the Apostles' days to our own has been a spreading and strengthening of the bonds which unite mankind together. There are painful problems in history,— such as the prevalence of destructive wars, and the dying out of inferior races before the stronger and more civilized. But the general result is a steady growth of humanity as a whole. We cannot comfort ourselves with the thought that the time has come for wars to cease in all the earth. There have been wars recently; there may again be wars before long. A free nation ought not to provoke war; but it ought not to be too luxurious and ease-loving to fight, if the occasion should arise. But, in spite of wars,— sometimes in a remarkable degree *by means of* wars,—mostly through a great and increasing complication of influences, we see the hindrances to human fellowship taken out of the way, and the friendly and intelligent intercourse of human souls spreading over the face of the globe. The worshippers of the Son of man should surely see in this progress of humanity a conspicuous sign of his coming and glory. If there is a King of men, desiring to bind them together in the bonds of a Divine polity with the cords of spiritual fellowship, is it not he who is acting, when old barriers between nations are broken down, when new possibilities and stimulants of intercourse are discovered, when in all most widely separated regions of the earth men are learning to rejoice together, to grieve together, and to hope together?

Are such reflections as these which I have been suggesting *too broad* to be compatible with faith in Christ as the Head of the Church, and as the Teacher and Judge of the individual conscience? Is there any inconsistency between the secular aspects of the world and of civilization which the study of history compels us to consider, and that thankful acknowledgment of redemption through the blood of the Cross upon which our private Christian life is founded? There is none, surely, if we are attracted and sustained by what is really Divine in the revelation of Christ. The principles of love, of sacrifice, of spiritual obedience and fellowship, of the blessed dependence of the souls of men upon him who made them,—these shine to us in the face of Jesus Christ, and these are not falsified, they are illustrated and glorified, by all that belongs to the real progress of humanity. There was never any Christian who took in with more joy of understanding as well as of heart and soul the plain Gospel of redemption than St Paul did; and in his writings we may trace sufficient indications that, instead of shrinking and shutting his eyes, he would have exulted in all discoveries which gave *expansion* to his thoughts and contemplations. To him it was a delight, it was food and nourishment to his adoration, to look back as far as he could see into past ages, to look forward into the ages of ages that were to come, to see how the barriers that included the chosen nation were broken down, and to observe the fulfilment of the prophecies which foretold that the God of truth and love would make himself known to all the ends of the earth and gather all nations into a spiritual unity under the one Lord.

And what we want in these later ages is a heartier and warmer faith in those principles of the Divine nature which were manifested and identified with our humanity in Jesus Christ the Crucified. Nothing has been discovered in the progress of ages, science and history and politics can tell us of nothing, more good and blessed than the Love of God in Christ. Nothing is now known as truly good, which may not be seen in its perfection in Christ. The believing Christian ought only to rejoice, not to be afraid, as the thoughts of men are widened with the process of the suns. There is enough still to make us grieve, enough to perplex and distress us and fill us with a not unworthy impatience. But the spread of light, of freedom, of equal justice, of human happiness, ought to touch us as a tribute to the Kingship of the Son of man. It is ours to claim every note and fruit of progress in the world as illustrating the Kingdom of Christ. It is ours to take care that no narrowness of those who glory in the name of Christ, no setting of the temporary form or of the imperfect conception above the perfect spirituality, shall hinder those who are moving towards the light from blessing the Sun of righteousness in whose wings is healing, and from advancing in his light to shine more and more unto the perfect day.

IV.

CHRIST AND MODERN KNOWLEDGE.

COLOSSIANS II. 3.—"In whom are hid all the treasures of wisdom and knowledge."

To St Paul and his first readers knowledge did not represent exactly the same class of things which it does to us. When St Paul speaks of knowledge in his Epistles, he frequently refers to speculations about the unseen world, to theories of creation, to accounts of "principalities and powers" which filled up the space between the visible world and God. Another great branch of the knowledge of those days was acquaintance with laws and traditions, such as the Jewish doctors possessed. Those speculations about the powers of the invisible world, and the learning which handed down ancient traditions, appeared to the Apostle of little value compared with the knowledge of Christ. But he taught not only that to know Christ was a more precious knowledge, but also that by learning Christ a man would come to understand more about the invisible world and the mysterious space between God and men, and about the meaning of sacred books and historical traditions, than if he devoted himself eagerly to the study of the current lore upon those subjects.

In our day, knowledge happily represents something much more solid and fruitful than it did in the New Testament age. I may speak of the knowledge with which we have to do as also consisting chiefly of *two* great branches. Of the one branch *Nature*, or the world around us, is the object; of the other, *Man*, with all that relates to human history. Whether you know much or little, you may perceive that your knowledge belongs to the one or the other of these great provinces. The world of *nature* comprises all that we study as to the laws of the outward universe,—such as the movements of this earthly globe and of the heavenly bodies with which our earth is connected, the properties of the things we manufacture, the growth of the plants we cultivate, the habits of the animals we keep. The world of *man* includes the principles of human life in all its developments,—the instincts, the feelings, the modes of reasoning, the mutual obligations, of the human race to which we belong; it therefore embraces all such subjects as those of history, politics, and morality. When we make progress in modern knowledge, we are learning something either about the world which surrounds man, or about man. The laws of nature are the matter of one kind of knowledge, the life of the human race is the matter of the other.

But is there not, for Christians, a *third* kind of

knowledge, surpassing the others in excellence and value,—the knowledge of God, and of Christ in whom God is revealed? I answer, that it may indeed be convenient, for certain purposes, to treat the knowledge of God, or Theology, as a third and distinct branch of knowledge. But I would rather say that God is *at the heart* of each of the two bodies of knowledge which I have already described. In studying nature, we are feeling after God; in studying the life of mankind, we arrive at God. In the laws and uses of nature, we trace the impress of the mind of him who creates and animates nature; in the history of man there is set for our contemplation the life of him in whom we see God perfectly revealed, and mankind perfectly represented. Nature will be best known to us, if studied as God's handiwork; mankind will be best known to us, if studied as God's acknowledged offspring. This is the doctrine which I desire now to illustrate.

I take what St Paul says concerning Christ with reference to the knowledge of his time, and claim it as true with reference to the far wider, more real, more satisfying, knowledge of our own time. To shew in any worthy or adequate manner that in Christ are now hid all the treasures of wisdom and knowledge, would be a far greater task than I propose to attempt. But, as faith in Christ has been too often divorced from a love of modern knowledge—believers in Christ being too distrustful and afraid of intellectual activity and scientific research, and votaries of science being sometimes induced to regard our old Christian faith as unfavourable, if not a positive obstacle, to the progress of knowledge,—I shall try to suggest to you some helps which those who wish to acquire knowledge may find in the contemplation of Christ.

Let us suppose that we fix our eyes upon Christ, the Word of the ,Father, the Beginning of Creation, the Head of the human race. We are at the same time directing thoughts of interest and curiosity towards the world around us, or towards mankind and their history. In what ways, let us ask, are our minds affected by the contemplation of Christ?

1. We gain, in the first place, *a sense of unity*.

Observation by itself suggests that all things are connected together. It shews us how a number of little facts are gathered into one by the conception of some law which they illustrate, how the smaller laws are seen to be dependent on some higher law, and how all the visible creation tends thus towards one common centre. But the observation which discovers this tendency to unity, this predominating principle of unity, is rather that of highly-educated minds than that of those who are beginning to learn. The ordinary mind, when it is awakened to a genuine curiosity, finds itself in the presence of a boundless and overwhelming multitude of facts. What naturally happens to us is, to pick up a bit of knowledge here, and another bit of knowledge there; to learn that the earth goes round the sun, that the steam from boiling water is irresistibly expansive, that there were emperors of Rome called Cæsar, that a glorious Reformation took place in the 16th century. Now thoughtful men,—those who really understand science and the discipline of the mind,—tell us that knowledge of this unorganized kind is all but useless; that it is of the very essence of real insight into things to perceive the connection of one fact with another, to learn the causes of things, and to accustom oneself to look for sequence and subordination, for real order and progress, everywhere.

Whoever believes in the Word of God as bringing all things into shape and holding them together, whoever accepts the Apostolic doctrine that through him who came forth from the Father all things were made, and without him was not anything made that was made,—is also a believer in a centre of creation, not merely imagined and unknown, but revealed, living, and Divine. To such a believer the wondrous order of the universe is an expression of the mind of God, the mysterious force which moves creation onwards is an energy of the will of God. Every recognition of the abiding order of the world around us to which the most enthusiastic philosopher can give utterance will be welcome and sound natural to one who believes that the Eternal and Absolute God speaks (not only once spoke but continues to speak) the world into its being by and through his Word.

I must not speak of the profound conceptions of science, and of the mysteries of the Divine nature, as if they were things within the easy grasp of every common mind. But I venture to think that even a school-boy or school-girl, who is taught to regard the Son of God as the Lord and Head of creation,—to whom such sayings as this, "To us there is but one God, the Father, of whom are all things, and we unto him, and one Lord Jesus Christ, by whom are all things, and we by him," are, if nothing more intelligible, at least sacred dogmas,—holds already the key to the oneness of the creation in his hands. He has not yet learnt how to apply the key. But he knows that the world is not a chaos, a mass of confusion, coming by chance. He knows the great truth, that *all things serve*. He knows that there will be an order for him to apprehend, as soon as he can find it out. He is fully prejudiced, so to speak, in favour of law and unity.

2. But further, in contemplating Christ we are considering a *moral* being; not one who may be described as merely the ultimate Law of all laws, but a person manifesting will and affections. And assuredly this is the prominent aspect of Christ to the Christian mind. We see in him the love of the Father declared. In him the Maker of the universe is revealed as essentially a righteous and loving Father.

One therefore who looks up to Christ inevitably gains the impression that *Love* is at work, and is supreme, in the universe. He has a *prejudice*, to use the word again, in favour of benevolence as a principle and motive in the existing order of things.

To the mere observer, the appearances of the world, considered with reference to this point, are puzzling. There are innumerable indications that the tendency of the arrangements according to which the course of things is ordered, is to produce well-being and happiness. No one who studies nature can resist the impression which these indications make upon him. But the observer honestly admits that there is something to be said on the other side. There is a dark side of nature as well as a bright side. There are hurricanes strewing their dreadful path with death and desolation, as well as fields which smile to the rain and the sunshine. The impartial observer must take note of lightning and tempest, of plague, pestilence and famine, of battle and murder, and of sudden death, when he wishes to estimate the impressions which the course of nature as a whole makes upon him. The Christian, also, must not blind himself to facts; he may explain them, or mark them as unexplained, but he ought to recognize them fairly. It is unquestionable however that we who believe in Christ as perfectly revealing the Maker of all things can entertain no doubt as to the supremacy of Love in the universe. If such a prepossession, if the conviction that Love is supreme, is a *hindrance* to the fair understanding of the phenomena of the world, we have no alternative but to admit that Christians are so far at a disadvantage for the acquisition of knowledge. Meditate on the character and life of the Son of God, as they are presented to us in the Gospels, and you cannot possibly conclude that the Almighty Ruler is partly kind and partly unkind, that his disposition is mixed of good will and malice. But happily, the more thoroughly the phenomena of the world are investigated, the more does it appear that all that is created, all that belongs most properly to the order and permanence of things, is perceptibly *good*. Let us therefore have no misgivings. Let us rejoice to believe that the secret of the Maker is with those who trust in his goodness. The prepossession which Christ produces in us as to the loving nature of the Father is a help and not a hindrance to us in learning anything about the course of things. So often is it found under a steady gaze of inquiry that apparent or transient evil is only a disguise of real and permanent good, that in cherishing a confidence in the Fatherly love of God we may be sure that we are following so far a right and successful method of investigation.

3. To take another step, the knowledge of Christ is a knowledge of evil as well as of good. Christ is not only the Love of God manifested; he is the Love of God in conflict with hatred and

rebellion, the Love of God suffering and submitting to evil, for the sake of a higher and completer conquest thereby to be effected. This is the peculiar mystery of the Cross of Christ; it is this which enters with the greatest power into the convictions of the true Christian, this which has in fact subdued the world to Christ.

Under the influence of this belief we cannot fail to look for *a purpose of redemption* in history and in nature. Christ teaches and constrains us to regard his Father as having an end in view, which end is the perfecting and setting free of his creation, the bringing of all things into a living order and harmony, unmarred by taint or discord;—and as working towards this end chiefly through a spiritual conflict with spiritual evil. The Gospel of Christ does not solve for us the problem of evil; it does not explain, to our satisfactory comprehension, how a thing which God hates should enter into and remain in a world which is wholly subject to God. But it instructs us how to regard evil. It bids us think nothing essentially evil except the perversion of the will, or *sin*. It helps us to see what varied and far-reaching disorder and misery flow from this primary source. It teaches us to strive against evil in all its forms through seeking a renewal and blessed submission, and freedom in submission, of the will. It gives us glorious hopes, by shewing the attractive influences of God's grace to our unruly but susceptible wills, and by bearing witness that God is working with us to accomplish his own glory through our redemption, and that our humble but hopeful part is to submit to his guidance and inspiration.

The faith in a Divine purpose of redemption running through the ages may be the occasion, as it no doubt has been, of many mistakes of interpretation. Good Christians have insisted upon seeing a judgment of God, pronouncing some particular sentence, in this event and in that. They have hastily assumed that the Eternal Father sees through their eyes. Against this danger earnest Christians need to be on their guard.

But we have good reason to maintain that this faith sheds the truest light on history and nature. It explains some of the greatest and most important facts. It shews how physical evil may be made to minister to moral good, so much as to reconcile our minds to the existence of such evil, though not to deter us from endeavouring to remove it. It explains human progress; it shews how men make mistakes in order that they may learn truth; how one man may benefit by the failures of other men, one generation by the failures of those which have preceded it. It sets before us an ideal consistent with all facts; it teaches us what we must do in order that we may all advance together towards that ideal. Does not the Cross of Christ aid all our studies, when it shews us God training mankind to universal sonship, preparing them to be blameless before him in love, and promising then, and not till then, to make all their outward conditions those of peace, enjoyment, and delight?

4. Scientific observers tell us, that whilst we may see an undeniable progress upwards and onwards both in nature and history, that progress is exceedingly gradual and slow. Now it is true that Christians have been impatient, and our Christianity does not altogether condemn impatience. There is something noble in the righteous impatience of good men and Christians. But this again has been the occasion of errors. The most earnest believers, crying "Make haste, O Lord, to help us;" "How long, O Lord, how long?" have been apt to make sure that the world was immediately and suddenly coming to an end. Better, this, than indolent and ignoble acquiescence in wrong and foulness and misery. But if the mind be fixed on Christ himself, it appears to me that a wondering sense of God's infinite *patience* is likely to possess us. We see how long God had waited before sending his Son, what gradual preparations went before his coming, with what modesty and smoothness the introduction of the marvellous life of the Son of God into the world's history was effected, what a very little seed was sown for the bringing forth of the tree which was to overshadow the whole earth. Then when Christ had been exalted, we see how patiently the Father commended him to the faith of mankind, what humble and natural instruments he employed, how he let this and that instinct and custom and passion resist almost as it pleased the diffusion of the blessed Gospel. The whole history of the Gospel, to this day, surely

teaches us, amongst other lessons, the patience of God. So that I would not admit that the Christian who has most truly studied the mind of God in Christ would be the most likely to rebel against those evidences of the gradual and continuous character of the Divine operations in Nature which science in these days so abundantly discloses.

Let me now mention one or two ways in which the contemplation of Christ ought powerfully to aid the cultivation of knowledge, without blending so directly with the processes of acquiring it.

5. Imagine a man to be thoroughly possessed by the belief that this whole round world is God's world; that God is not merely above it, but in it. Let him believe with St Paul that "there is one God and Father of all, who is above all and through all and in all," that "of him, and through him, and unto him, are all things;"—with St John, that "God has created all things, and for his pleasure they are, and were created." Let him be exercised in the conviction that "the invisible things of God from the creation of the world are clearly seen, being understood by the things that are made." Do you not take it as certain, that in proportion as such a man knows God through Christ and loves and worships him, he will feel drawn both by encouragement and by obligation to the study of the things which, as he believes, God is actually making and doing? No doubt every person cannot give his mind to every thing. Many of us are so busy with necessary labours

that we have no time for anything like study, whether of nature or of the human sciences. But, of two men in the same circumstances and with the same opportunities, surely the one who honours Christ the most will prize knowledge the most, and will have the most lively interest in learning. Where another man will be thinking chiefly of getting on in the world by the powers which knowledge supplies, or of making himself superior through culture to his neighbours, the simple and loyal Christian will remember that in all study he has to do with the works and ways of his Lord, and that by reverent consideration of those works and ways he may get nearer to the very mind of God himself. I do not stop to speak now of the comparative value of different objects of knowledge, because my point is, that with regard to any and every kind of knowledge, the Christian has a peculiar reason, in the homage he pays to Christ, for taking an interest in it. He is the more bound by duty to know; he has a higher reward in knowing.

6. Lastly, the moral discipline that belongs to the contemplation of Christ is favourable to the acquisition of knowledge. The pursuit of knowledge—as who does not know?—has many hindrances to contend with. Not chill penury alone has been the cause, with multitudes of men, that

> "Knowledge to their eyes her ample page,
> Rich with the spoils of time, did ne'er unroll;"

but indifference and laziness, bluntness to higher things, love of money or of personal display, have kept them ignorant and stupid. In these days, even the poor have wonderful opportunities for self-culture and for gaining knowledge, if only they care in earnest to avail themselves of them. Now Christianity certainly places the spirit and the affections first, and will dignify a simple man who is true and loyal to Christ more than a well-educated man who is ungodly. But it places the mind above the flesh. The flesh and its lusts it bids us keep down and bring into subjection. It habitually raises the thoughts above the level of sensual enjoyments and vanities. It strengthens the resolution, making a man strong to do what is right and worthy and not merely what is pleasant for the moment. And it cultivates the habits of docility and truthfulness. Christ taught that those who would follow him must become like a little child,—that is, teachable and truthful. And this is the mind for acquiring knowledge. It has been said indeed that *scepticism* is a most necessary habit for one who would ground himself in real knowledge, because he must be always ready to doubt whether what he now believes is true. But then this scepticism is not levity or conceit, but really another name for teachableness and truthfulness. No doubt he who reverences truth must always be ready to abandon a cherished error. But this is a Christian disposition; and the better Christian a man is, the more gladly will he submit to be corrected when he is wrong.

These, my Christian brethren, are some of the

links or influences through which our faith in Christ will rightly act upon our pursuit of knowledge.

I must not be tempted to illustrate my subject further. But suffer me, in conclusion, to urge upon you a twofold exhortation.

1. In seeking and increasing knowledge, endeavour, if you feel the truth of what I have been saying, to keep Christ always in view. This contemplation will not render your minds less open to the reception of new truths when they are disclosed to you. Some of you may remember indeed that there have been conflicts of a long and even bitter character between the champions of some new discoveries of science and the believers in the letter of Scripture. There is, we must admit, a danger of such conflicts, where the letter of Scripture is exalted to the place which Christ, and Christ alone, should occupy in the worship of the Christian. The Holy Scriptures are of inexpressible value, if it were only for this reason, that without them we should have no secure knowledge of Christ. But the loyalty of the Christian is due principally to Christ; and if his loyalty to Christ is ever brought into apparent collision,—as it has been more than once in the progress of knowledge,—with the letter of Scripture, it is the letter of Scripture and not Christ, the Lord of life and light, that must give way. And I have no fears or misgivings in urging you, as you seek to know more and more, to keep your eyes fixed as much as possible on Christ. He will be your best guide.

He will exalt and purify your intellectual tone. He will purge your mind of vanity, of selfish rivalry, of that irreverence towards knowledge of which we are guilty when we degrade it into a mere stepping-stone for worldly advancement.

2. Secondly, in your character and endeavours as Christians, in your zeal for Christ, do not despise modern knowledge. Speaking of the Christian world generally, for generations and centuries. I am afraid it must be said that the most zealous Christians have not given the aid and impulse which they ought to have given and which it was in their power to give, to the advancement of knowledge. Why has there been this defect? I would not say that it has been through want of sincerity in love to Christ: but then it must have been through some want of appreciation of Christ's true majesty or sovereignty, through want of full *confidence* in him as the Life and Light of men. May we be on our guard against this narrowness! We have need to be watchful. There is a certain temptation to some minds to throw themselves into religion, and in doing so to put aside the thoughts and inquiries of the age as secular and as likely to breed scepticism. I might dwell on the folly, the impolicy, of a religion allied to ignorance, of an attempt to shut out by mere will the suggestions of doubt. But I now venture to speak to you in a higher strain; I say that such rejection of knowledge is in fact, though people may not be aware of it, disloyal to Christ. Not only is Christ not afraid

of the diffusion of knowledge and inquiry; it is he who gives the knowledge and stimulates the inquiry. If there are any beliefs in which we have been brought up, to which the light of advancing knowledge makes it impossible to us to cling, who is it that bids us give them up? Not some godless spirit of the age, but the Lord Jesus Christ himself. It is surely the vocation of us who live in these days (might God only make us worthy of it and true to it!) to rise out of and above bondage to systems and the letter into the freedom of fellowship with the Son of God himself. Depend upon it, we need for this, not a light spirit of incredulity and doubt, but a stronger and surer faith. Our faith needs to be proved and tested and braced. Seek then and promote knowledge without reserve, I say not *although* you believe in Christ, nor will I say only *because* you believe in him, but also *in order* that you may believe in him more surely.

V.

HUMANITY AND THE TRINITY.

St John xvii. 20, 21.—"Neither pray I for these alone, but for them also which shall believe on me through their word; that they all may be one; as thou, Father, art in me, and I in thee, that they also may be one in us."

This day is our festival of the Unity of the Godhead. The question to which our faith gives an answer to-day is this: Will we have *three* Gods, or *two* Gods,—or will we have *One God?* And our Christian answer is the same as that of the Hebrew worshippers of old, "The Lord our God is *One Lord.*"

At other times rather than to-day we ask ourselves, Whether we confess Jesus of Nazareth, the Crucified, to be the risen and exalted Son of God; and whether we recognize a Divine Spirit proceeding from the Father and the Son, given to be the higher life of men. When the special doctrine of the Trinity comes before us, it invites us to consider, Whether we, believers in Christ,—we, believers in the Spirit of Christ and of the Father,—are also believers in One only God.

It is the glory and the difficulty of our faith to believe in Unity. To believe in more Gods than One, is easy and natural. The heathen, ancient and modern, have believed most frankly and liberally in many gods. They have worshipped a god in the firmament, another in the immense ocean, another in the under world. They have named a sun-god, and a moon-goddess. They have had national gods, gods of Egypt, of Assyria, of Greece, of Italy. But Christians have not been exempt from the same tendency. They have worshipped Christ, the peculiar God of Christendom; with him they have confessed a distant universal Father; they have added a goddess, in the Virgin-Mother, to the heavenly court; and they have paid homage to tutelary divinities in angels and glorified saints. And in this distributed worship Christians have at times lost all thought and care about unity. Can it be said that philosophers, who have set themselves free with more or less of scorn from heathen and Christian modes of polytheism, are able to attain easily to a real faith in Unity? Are they not tempted to make gods variously and in combination, of Force and Matter, of Nature, Humanity, Art, Fate?—As Christians, we confess the mystery of the Divine Unity; we do not call this Unity a simple idea which you can grasp as easily as you can name it; we hold that we need to be led up to it, and that unless we are sustained at a height above that of our merely natural conceptions, we fall as a matter of course into the worship of divided powers; we believe that we approach the most absolute Unity in the universe by allowing the Son to be the way for us to the Father, and by contemplating the fellowship of the Son and of the Father till our minds and our imaginations fail before a task to which they know themselves to be unequal.

The Divine Unity, then, is the object towards which our thoughts and devotions are now directed. As one way of observing what needs are satisfied by the Christian doctrine of the Divine Unity, let us endeavour to take a glance at *Humanity* as a whole, so as to see how it is bound up both with each Divine Person, and with One God. By humanity I mean mankind, the race and nature of man, the whole, of which we ourselves are members.

1. And, first, consider that in humanity there is a *filial heart* which delights to confess and to call upon a *Divine Father*.

In Christendom this may be said to be a *cultivated* rather than a *natural* instinct. And in all the best religions, it has been made a duty and a privilege to believe that there is in heaven or the unseen world some kind of counterpart of earthly fatherhood, some being to whom thanks and vows and entreaties may be offered.

But in the most degraded races and under the tyranny of the wildest superstitions this filial instinct can hardly be said to be ever entirely wanting. In all countries you may perceive rudiments or vestiges of it. Where the fatherhood that can be seen, the earthly human fatherhood, is a relation defaced by carelessness and cruelty and caprice, there the invisible world will hold no worthy image of Divine

Fatherhood. But it is scarcely possible to imagine a race,—it would be quite impossible, I believe, to find one,—which would not have at least some flickering notions of providence, of invisible guidance, of a power which has given, of a power from which benefits may be hoped.

The filial instinct may no doubt appear to be all but wanting in some populations. It may be said perhaps to be unknown in the inhabitants of the Andaman islands. But the human beings who are without it are those who are scarcely human. We may call it an essentially human instinct for this reason, that it grows with the growth of humanity. Where humanity itself is cultivated, there the sense of a Divine Fatherhood becomes stronger, and the image of that Fatherhood becomes purer. In Persia, in Greece, in Italy,—to mention countries with which we do not associate the idea of a special revelation,—not only did men look up to the heavenly world with filial instincts, that is to say, with gratitude, trust, and hope, with belief in a heavenly order and beneficence, but the name of Father, as applied to a supreme God, became distinct and dear and sacred. The most perfect worship of the Father is that which the New Testament teaches, and which has in varying but always imperfect degrees been realized in Christendom. And even those to whom the Christian revelation is no more than a dream of man's excited imagination are ready to admit that the faith of Christ has been allied with all that is best in human progress, and that the Christian nations have been in fact the most *humane* amongst the nations of mankind.

Looking at the history and experience of individuals, you may see that the truly filial nature is best developed in those whom you regard and revere the most. The spirit which lives as in response to the manifestation of a just and wise and loving Father is the best kind of human spirit you know. And those who try to live in this mind think themselves to be living most worthily when they are most fully governed by such a spirit. They condemn themselves with the most assurance and shame when they are unfilial towards God; they find their purest happiness, their most wholesome vital element, in humility, in gratitude, in faith and hope and love.

May we not say then with confidence that humanity by its very nature seeks for and demands a Divine Father, and when at its best goes forth most joyfully in filial utterances towards a Father?

Tell men that this faith in a Father is nothing but a superstitious reflexion of that relation between Father and children which happens to be a law of human existence. Tell them that science, upon which alone it is safe to build, reveals no Father in heaven to whom they may cry. Offer to them, instead, *a course of things* in which they and all things are moving onwards, a *Nature* originating in no Will, tending to no desired end, only going on and on, blindly, deafly, dumbly, inexorably. Bid them repress as childish follies all gratitude for mercies received, all desire of mercies to come. Would you in this way feed and nourish the universal humanity that is in men? Does our human nature feel comforted and bettered by such prescriptions? Does it not on the contrary feel starved as by cold and hunger? Where would, in such a case, be the refuge of the solitary prisoner, of the reformer striving with an evil generation, of every man when things go against him, unless indeed he were able to find his satisfaction in a sublime self-complacency?

2. Secondly, I would suggest that, when we endeavour to regard mankind as a whole, we are constrained to look for some Head, some Pattern and Ideal, some Centre *to give unity to the members* which make up the whole. The human race needs a more-than-human Son of man, in whom it may find and become conscious of its unity.

This need will not, I am aware, be so evident to you as that cry to a Divine Father which issues out of the heart of universal humanity. But it is worth our while to consider it a little.

We should not willingly abandon our belief in the unity of the human race. This idea grows upon men as they rise and advance. An improved morality implies and strengthens it. Not only the Christian faith, but also every higher and nobler conviction, compels us to feel that we are united in a peculiar manner to our brother-men, that every man has a claim upon us because he is a man, that we are members of one body. But on what does this faith rest? The researches of science, especially in recent years, have had some tendency to weaken and dissolve it. Science shews us human beings whom it is dreadfully hard to recognize as brother-men; it has made it almost certain that through unmeasured ages races of men have existed in conditions not much raised above those of the brutes; it brings into view the likenesses which exist between the animal nature of man and that of the inferior creatures; it exhibits relentlessly the painful phenomena of disease and death, and compels us to confess the dependence of the mind and of the character upon the body. Science breaks through any line with which we may hope to round off into a compact and creditable whole this creation of the human race; it gives a ragged edge, a blurred outline, to any image of the human race which may have presented itself to our minds. We are not likely to strengthen ourselves in the belief of the unity of mankind by looking, so to speak, to the *circumference*, and assuring ourselves that in *that* there is no breach. But if we can look to a *centre*, it will not be so necessary for us to define the circumference. If we can discern a perfect Head, we need not be so much troubled by any imperfections in the extremities.

And this is the key which our Christian faith gives us to the unity of mankind. Why are we brother-men, fellow-members of one body? Because we are a Divine family, having a Divine Head and Elder Brother. We are all imperfect, we are all unworthy; the Divine image is not perfectly traced in any of us. Who is to say by what *degree* of imperfection and unworthiness man's fellowship with the Son of man is broken? We renounce the attempt to determine it. We do not know from what beginning, from what ruins, the Living Head may be able to raise or restore a member. We know that, in looking to the Divine Son of man, we learn to look upon ourselves and our brother-men most reverently. In confessing him, the bond which unites us to one another becomes most undeniable and most sacred. Can you suppose that any other ruling conception than that of a Divine and human Head would have wrought out in the mind of St Paul that sublime theory of human fellowship and mutual responsibility which has ever since been the actual basis of Christian morality?—I say then, that in order to preserve a high ideal and a substantial conviction of human unity, we want such a being as the Christ of whom the Gospel bears witness to us. Those who acknowledge him need no other proof that they and all men are rightly called brethren. Christ claiming men as related to him declares them to be all related to one another. The Christian faith in human fellowship and unity may find support and illustration in every token and symptom of community of race or identity of nature which inquiry or experience may discover. But if we depend on such signs *alone*, we shall have to balance arguments from likeness against arguments from unlikeness. What we read about development and variation of species will give us an uneasy feeling that moral unity is a mere phantom, and that we know nothing of our nature except that some creatures by happy circumstances have worked forward or been pushed forward, farther than others. Consciousness of responsibility would no doubt by some means or other survive: but it is difficult to see on what basis it can firmly rest, or by what contemplations it can be nourished. If we are to look upon our kind as an ordered host moving steadily though slowly forward, and advancing by rational and conscious effort, we must have some leader; there must be one to whom all may attach themselves, whom all may follow.

And thus the higher idea of humanity bears witness to him in whose likeness we are created and by whose government we are kept together.

3. Thirdly, the common emotions and affections which make the higher life of humanity point to a more than human *Spirit* breathing one breath into men's souls.

As we are one body, so we are made to drink into one Spirit.

The better life of men is expressly non-selfish. When we are at our best, and most conscious of our unity, we are also entering into feelings which are higher than those which belong to us as merely separate individuals, into feelings which we recognize as common to our race or kind, feelings which are contagious as well as elevating. When we yield ourselves to harmony and mutual service, we know that we are raised by a spirit to which we inwardly do homage, we rejoice in it without pride or self-complacency. We *count upon* such a common elevating spirit. We are sure that other men may be roused and wakened by it. In our exhortations and rebukes, in our sympathy and in our appeals to sympathy, we imply a common spiritual atmosphere, in which we live and move and have our being. Is it easy to interpret these experiences, these demands, without plainly confessing a heavenly Spirit, which is the better life of our common humanity?

Consider also, brethren, that we know ourselves most certainly, and see our fellow-men most plainly, to be animated by a better Spirit than that which belongs to each man in himself, in those moments when filial piety to the Divine Father, and loyalty to the Divine Head, are strongest. Human beings, of any race or country, are raised above themselves then most, when they are truest to the Father and to the Son. What is this, but that the Spirit of the Father and of the Son takes possession of human hearts; that there is a true Spirit of the Divine family, by whose inspiration men feel and act upon their sonship and their brotherhood?

The human dwellers upon this round earth are greatly *separated* by differences of habits and associations and culture, as well as by the more obvious barriers of language. The thoughts of grown-up persons are not the thoughts of children; the thoughts of highly educated and civilized Europeans are not the thoughts of untutored savages.

It is difficult to make a bridge from one sort of intellectual conceptions to another sort. But kindness, love, devotion, reverence, form a language of hearts in which any human beings find it in some degree practicable to converse with any other human beings. Faith, hope, charity, these three, not only *abide*, through successions of changes; they also spread over the whole surface of humanity. They are not only permanent, they are also universal. And these are the breath of the One Divine Spirit, and always come most readily into the soul when they are sought and thankfully received as gifts from above.

Mankind, then, to be *livingly* and *spiritually one*, wants a Spirit which can impart a worthy common life, such a Spirit as that which came on the day of Pentecost from the Father and the Son.

What I have been endeavouring to say concerning the whole of mankind, may find illustrations in *any portion* of mankind. We here,—to take ourselves now gathered in this Church for an example,—if we hear the voice of our common humanity speaking strongly within us, are moved to call upon one Father above us, to look to one Lord, to open our hearts to one Spirit. And then we feel our unity most deeply and cordially; then the powers which bind us in one prove themselves stronger than the powers which separate us.

But if we are thus made ideally and practically one by the joint confession of the Father, the Son, and the Holy Spirit, there cannot be separateness in the *objects of our worship*. Father, Son, and Holy Spirit, must be one also. There can be but One God. And his unity is not that of singleness and isolation; it is that of a fellowship, passing understanding, of the Father and Son in the Spirit.

The early Church was led gradually to the confession of a threefold Unity in the Godhead. The first Christians were worshippers of Christ. Christ was a God to them, obviously the object of a far more adoring homage than ever heathen god was to any of his worshippers. None the less, so long as they were true to Christ himself, were they worshippers of *the Father*. The question did not force itself upon them at first, hardly in New Testament times; but it could not help coming,—Did the believers in Jesus Christ worship two Gods, or One? They answered to themselves, that they *must* believe in One God; that they could not give up their faith in Christ. What then was the issue? *The fellowship of the Father and of the Son*, as they contemplated it, became infinitely and mysteriously *close*. They became convinced that that fellowship might most rightly be described by the name *Unity;* and that the Father, the Son, and the Spirit of the Father and of the Son, were to be worshipped and invoked as one incomprehensible God.

We are led along the same path by the order of our Church seasons. Christ is kept continually before us, Christ as the Son revealing the Father, Christ as uniting us to himself and bearing our sins. We follow Christ up to the heaven from which he came. We remember the coming down of the Spirit to create a new common life, higher and more heavenly than had before been known upon earth. And then we are cautioned by the recurrence of this day not to forget that we are believers in *One God*, not to allow ourselves to offer divided homage to three separate Beings. The Son is to lead us to the Father; and the Father, with the Son and the Spirit, is to be One God to us, blessed for evermore.

But, this morning, I have been endeavouring to lead your minds by another track to the same goal. I have been inviting you to observe how Humanity, with its higher voices and aspirations, seeks and answers to a common Father, a common Head, a common Spirit. The glory and perfection of mankind is in its unity: but how is its unity to be understood and to be realized? Not by merely studying human beings as they are and as they have been, and shutting the eyes to all that is above them: but by consenting to see the heavenly invisible bonds which draw them upwards, which hold them together, which lead them onwards.

If we, brethren, are permitted to discern however dimly with the eye of faith these nobler affinities of our human nature, may we have grace to yield ourselves to them and to rejoice in them! If we know ourselves to be more than earthly, more than animal, let us take care that we rise in heart and spirit above the cares and interests and limitations of earth, above the sway of animal passions! The doctrine of an absolute Divine Unity subsisting in the spiritual fellowship of a Father and of a Son lays a strong hand of obligation upon our spirits. It bids us look everywhere for signs of fatherhood, of filial obedience, of spiritual fellowship. It bids us strive that our own lives may be conformed to the constitution of our common humanity; that in all things we may be followers and worshippers of unity; that we may be true to the Father, to Christ, and to the Holy Ghost; that we may overcome all the influences around us and from beneath which would separate us from one another and from our God.

VI.

NATURE.

Psalm VIII. 1.—"O Lord our Governor, how excellent is thy name in all the world; thou that hast set thy glory above the heavens!"

The present age, dating now from some time back, has been remarkable for scientific discovery. In all departments of inquiry, knowledge has been greatly advanced and purified. It is especially, perhaps, in theories concerning the surface of the earth on which we tread, and concerning the history of mankind, that common opinion has been modified. By observing the character of the strata or layers which, one below another, make the crust of this round earth, and by bringing together the remains of life which are found in those strata, geologists have been able to arrive at conclusions as to the antiquity and order and physical aspects of great periods in the earth's history, which men have been slow and unwilling to receive, but the proofs of which have become practically irresistible. In the history of the countries and races of mankind, partly by the discovery of new sources of knowledge, partly by the better sifting and comparing of the old, many received opinions have been shewn to be erroneous, and many new vistas have been opened which begin with being clear and definite and reach gradually through the obscure to the utterly impenetrable and unknown. This progress of knowledge has given much food and excitement to the minds of men. Inquiry and speculation have been stimulated; intellectual ambition has been rewarded by a sense of ampler possession and genuine conquest. The sphere of intelligent wonder has been immensely enlarged. If with such knowledge as men had between two and three thousand years ago a contemplative mind felt constrained to cry out to the Creator, "O Lord, how manifold are thy works! in wisdom hast thou made them all: the earth is full of thy riches!"—it is certain that the wealth and complexity and mystery of the Divine works are now indefinitely multiplied.

And no doubt the growing insight into the variety and relations and unity of the Divine works has been accompanied by much lifting up of the heart in pious admiration and reverence to God. But it is also true that the progress of science has had some effect in confusing and blunting the old instincts of piety towards the Creator. Old-fashioned religion and new-fashioned science have been led to take even hostile attitudes towards one another. Scientific men have accused religion of being blind and bigoted; religious men have accused science of being presumptuous and irreverent. There are two characteristics of modern discovery, as indeed of all discovery, which have been the chief occasion of this lamentable opposition. One is the increased proof of the presence and regularity of laws of nature; the other is the pushing back of origins into obscurity. That these results have come from inquiry is indisputable. Whenever, and in whatever direction, knowledge has grown, the presence of law has been in some way made manifest, and some limit which had been set for a beginning has been pushed back. With regard to this latter point, I am not speaking of *time* merely. In all countries tradition has been free with numbers in chronology as in other reckonings; and rigid inquiry has proved that things supposed to be thousands of years old must date their age by hundreds. But where beginnings have been described, —by saying that this or that came first into existence in such a way, and that it was due to such and such causes,—it is found, I think I may say invariably, that when more light is thrown upon the supposed origin, we see that what appeared to be sudden was in fact gradual, that earlier forms of the same thing and remoter causes come into view, and the origin, therefore, instead of being fixed at a certain point, is pushed further and further back. Now if religion has taught us to say, " The Creator works his will in the universe, and it is his glory to do just what he pleases without regard to rule;" and, " the Creator suddenly projected certain forms of life, certain events, certain epochs of history into existence, without relation to what went before, by a fiat of his sovereign will,"—it is inevitable that when all phenomena are seen increasingly to be ordered by law, and when the boundaries of abrupt creation tend to disappear, the ordinary utterances of our piety should seem to be impeded. And to some extent this has been the case. We have been accustomed,—and perhaps it could not have been helped,—to associate our thoughts of God rather with interference than with the giving forth and sustaining of law, and rather with instantaneous creation than with gradual evolution, and therefore we are not ready at once to assimilate with our reverence for God the beautiful and profound revelations of God's work which have been made to modern science.

I do not suppose that it is within any one's power to explain the mysteries of Divine operation in the universe, so that the freedom of God (or of man either) shall seem easily reconcilable with the fixity of laws, or so that God's leading of the ages may naturally commend itself to every eye as the secret of the evolutions of history. It seems to me that in striving after the solution of such problems we soon reach the limits not only of our actual but of our possible knowledge, and that we become in a strange and instructive manner conscious of the inadequacy of our faculties.

But we may endeavour to put ourselves in such a position that problems which we cannot solve may not hinder our faith and worship more than they ought to do. Now, according to all reason and all Scriptural example, the most devout believer in

God, the most earnest Christian, ought to rejoice with the most natural delight in the expansion of knowledge, and the more God's works are unfolded and explained the more ought he to admire the Creator's wisdom. We have admitted that, in consequence of certain difficulties, it is not universally true that in proportion to a man's genuine piety is his delight in the revelations of science. I suppose, then, the question to be asked, How may we best seek for the true pious feeling towards the wonders of nature and the world? And as a partial answer to such a question, I wish to call your attention to one principle.

Our knowledge of God, and our interest in God's works and ways, should *begin*, not with the beginning of the Creation, nor with the phenomena of the external world, but with the present relations of God to our spirits, to ourselves personally and to mankind. What is God to us, and what are we to God? These are the questions which concern us most closely. If we can attain to a clear and firm faith on these points, we may be content to remain in some ignorance as to the *mode* of God's working in nature. The trust and love which are based upon our own spiritual relations with God, will not depend upon our settling how the laws of nature are made to serve the will of God, but will overflow, as it were, upon the outward world, will be ready to accommodate themselves thankfully to whatever science may disclose to us.

It would be a great mistake to infer from the

order of the books in the Bible, and from Genesis coming first, that the natural and appointed way of knowing God is to know him first as the Creator of the visible universe, and then to advance to the knowledge of him as our own Lord and Father. As a matter of fact, we may easily satisfy ourselves that this has never been the progress of men's faith in God. God is the God of the conscience first; afterwards he is the God of the heavens and of the earth.

Take the case of the Israelites themselves, whose sacred books the ancient Scriptures were. In what character was God first and chiefly known to them? As Jehovah, the God of the Covenant, the God of Abraham, Isaac, and Jacob. The young Israelite was taught, as soon as he was able to learn, that he was the subject of a righteous King, whose laws he was bound to obey. By this righteous King his race had been called out and claimed. Jehovah had been the Friend and Guide of his fathers, and by a series of mighty acts had delivered the people of Israel, and made a nation of them. The absolute allegiance of every Israelite was due to a Lord who was not to be confounded with any outward or visible thing. Worship of outward and visible things was a crime against the invisible Lord. Jehovah was the Lord of visible things, and he desired the children of the chosen seed to be also spiritually masters of visible things. He bade them serve him and be true to him apart from any relations with outward things; and he then promised to reward with outward things those who in spirit were loyal to him.

This was the primary religious education of every Israelite. He was not insensible, any more than the neighbouring nations, to the fascination of the outward world. The sun in his splendour and the moon in her beauty might have been gods to him as to others. But his mind was called off from these to the contemplation of the righteous Lord. To know and to worship Jehovah, the righteous one, the Redeemer, the Lawgiver, the God of the people,—this was the religion of the Israelite. In proportion as he was saved from idols and was a true worshipper of Jehovah, he was himself raised above visible things and enabled to assert his own spiritual lordship. This being the most important matter, the Jew was likely to ask, and he was not discouraged from asking, What are these wonderful and beautiful things around us, by which our life is so much affected, though we may not yield to them and serve them, these things upon which we ourselves can exert some modifying force? And the answer given to him was, These things are the works of Jehovah, not equal in dignity to man, but yet his real products, the instruments of his will, and subject to his gracious disposition for the training and blessing of men. God made these, and therefore they are wonderful and glorious: but he made man in his own image, and he intends *them* to serve man.

I have alluded to the fact that other races made

gods of the wonderful objects and powers of the natural world. But in all heathen nations the religion of the conscience has taken precedence of the religion of mere nature. If they have hardly known the righteous Lord, men have made for themselves in their own image arbitrary gods, not passionless physical powers, but gods who might be offended and propitiated, beings of will and purpose. They have thus confessed the ascendancy of the spiritual over the physical. And the more clearly and firmly they have made this confession, the more they have been themselves elevated; whereas those who have thought of human beings as only items and portions of the physical world, and have asserted no dominion over and little rebellion against the natural forces, have been also the most degraded and least progressive of mankind.

What is the testimony of our own Scriptures, the Scriptures of the New Covenant, in this matter? If we are to look upon this volume as the book of a religion (which is not a very good account of it), we find hardly any attempt to explain the relations of either God or man towards the physical universe and the powers and laws of nature. The books of the New Testament are the books of a spiritual Kingdom, a Kingdom revealed in Christ, and having for its sphere the spiritual natures of men. Jesus Christ, the Son of God, manifests and declares the Father. By his death and resurrection he founds a Kingdom in which men are brought near to their Father in heaven. The Apostles go forth to proclaim this Kingdom, and their Master the Lord of it, and to invite men to enter into it and be thereby saved. The high spiritual and human importance of the Gospel would naturally make all questions relating to the physical world comparatively insignificant to those who were charged with the first promulgation of the Gospel. Accordingly, in the New Testament we find scarcely a single allusion to the earliest history of the world or of mankind. The Apostles do not seem to have felt the necessity of going back to the first chapters of Genesis, to the origin of things or to the fall of man. Adam is mentioned by St Paul in two important passages, where he is the Representative of the sinfulness and mortality of the human race, in contrast with Christ the Representative of its true sonship and restoration to life. But these are philosophical passages rather than plain historical or didactic statements. The sin from which the Apostles preached a salvation was the actual sin bearing miserable fruits of death around them; they bade men be saved by trusting in Christ and in the Father through him. They probably thought little, and therefore said little, about the sun and moon and stars, about the beasts or the grass of the field.

In a broad but decisive and significant manner, *all things* are referred in the New Testament to the power and will of God, and in particular to that Word of God which was made flesh in Jesus Christ. This was undoubtedly a part of the primary and fundamental faith of the Christian, whether any further explanation could be given or not. "Of him and through him and unto him are all things." "To us there is one God the Father, of whom are all things." "To us there is one God the Father, of whom are all things, and we unto him; and one Lord Jesus Christ, by whom are all things, and we by him." "One God and Father of all, who is above all, and through all, and in all." "In him we live and move and are." "Thou hast created all things, and for thy pleasure they exist, and were created." "The Word was in the beginning with God: all things were made through him, and without him was not anything made that was made."

These and the like are familiar statements in the New Testament, and they illustrate the position of the first Christians, as believers in Christ, towards the universe which surrounded them. Christ and his redemption, Christ revealing the Father, are the leading objects of thought; and to Christ all things are subject. The following passage from St Paul sums up the Apostolic doctrine: "Giving thanks to the Father, who has enabled us to be partakers of the inheritance of the saints in light; who has delivered us from the power of darkness, and has transferred us into the kingdom of the Son of his love; in whom we have redemption through his blood, the forgiveness of sins: who is the image of the invisible God, the firstborn of all creation: for by him were all things created, that are in heaven and that are in earth, visible and invisible, whether they be thrones or dominions or principalities or powers, all things were created by him and for him, and he is before all things, and in him all things consist, or are held together."

But whilst there is this breadth and firmness, but at the same time absence of detail and speculation, in what the New Testament says about the external world, we may remember that there are narratives in the New Testament which are referred to in almost every discussion about the laws of nature. These are the *miracles*, whether of our Lord, or of his servants. These have been stumblingblocks to many of the observers of the uniformity of natural processes. It belongs to my present purpose to observe that these acts undoubtedly represent our Lord as claiming a mastery over the powers of nature, and that when we consider them, instead of being arbitrary interferences with the natural course of things, we perceive them to fit in very remarkably with the more ordinary course of things as influenced and wrought upon by spiritual force. No one can deny that spiritual force, operating by the human will, produces changes and brings about designed results, in the natural world; and the mighty works recorded in the New Testament are far more analogous to this action than to the marvels which the human imagination has been accustomed to crave and to invent. The proper effect of these miracles is rather to give us a feeling that Divine will behind the veil can make the laws of nature subservient to its ends, than to make us think of nature as going on by fate and of God as sometimes interfering with nature.

If then we are to follow such guidance as is given us in both the Old and the New Testaments, we shall treat, I venture to say, all difficulties and problems about the laws of nature and the antiquity of the world and of the human race as insignificant compared with the great truths of our relation to Christ and to the Father in the Spirit. Here, in these truths, is what is most essential; and here also we must look to find the principles by which other relations are to be interpreted. Our own education in the Church is founded on this basis. In the Catechism we learn first, and we learn last too, what God has made us to himself, what relations he has established between us and him by the sending of his Son. The Catechism teaches our children nothing about beginnings, nothing about miracles, nothing about the mode of the Divine operations in the Universe. It affirms plainly that God has made us and all things: but it speaks chiefly of our sacred calling, of the Divine manifestation in Christ, of the will and commandments of God, of our privileges and our duty. These are the things in which all Christians are to be grounded. Let us take care to give these their due precedence.

If we do, it will certainly follow that we cannot regard any of the discoveries of science, however wonderful and however useful, as competing in importance or dignity with what God has revealed to us in the Gospel. It is a greater thing to know that we and all mankind have been redeemed from sin and death, and that we may take up the position of reconciled children of the righteous and merciful Father, and that we have a Spirit given us, working in us and our brethren as a spirit of love and sanctification, who is the Spirit of the Father and of the Son, than to have all the knowledge of all the philosophers. If this is presumption, it is a presumption of which our Christianity makes us guilty, and we should be false to our faith in consenting to take a lower position.

But, when we have thus believed concerning God and ourselves,—when we have exalted what is purely spiritual above all that is merely physical, —may we not be the better prepared to see in physical things the instruments and the vestures of spirit? We can learn in part from our own experience how closely the outward and visible creation may be connected with spirit. Our bodies, the works of our hands,—how they are moulded by our spirits, how much they reveal of our spirits! So then this world around us, made by him who is the Father of our spirits, how much may it not tell us of him! We shall surely look upon it not only with respect, but with an inquiring and teachable mind. What is going on now, by the operation of natural forces guided by natural laws,—what we can learn from relics and natural records to have gone on in former ages and periods,—if we can understand it, must tell us something of the mind and purpose of God. The very Word of God, of whom St John speaks, is to be partially read in it. If we can suppose St Paul or St John to have been living in the light of modern science, we cannot believe indeed that they would have been persuaded to think less of the primary all-transcending importance of their Gospel; but we may well imagine that they would have found much more to attract them, much more to reward their study, in the laws which have already been discovered and which men of science are still feeling after, than they had to tempt them in their own unscientific age. Natural science cannot of itself find out God or declare God; God has been otherwise made known to us. We could not rise by natural stepping-stones from the Creator to the Father and Redeemer. But if we will descend, so to speak, from the Father to the Creator, from God in Christ to God in Nature, we may find the whole world endowed with new voices of testimony and revelation.

Let this be our hope and faith. When we look abroad on the scenes of heaven and earth, and say, "Our Father made them all," let us not be content with a mere unintelligent survey. Where God has wrought, that which is most subtle, most inward, that which is the law and secret of things, is more Divine than the mere surface which strikes the eye. Let us be grateful therefore to men of science, and so far as we have opportunities let us be glad to enter into their labours. We may most of us have no choice but to remain ignorant of much that they know, but we need none of us disparage or denounce the knowledge we are obliged to forego. There can be no lie written upon God's creation. In their own way all his works praise him; though only his saints can give thanks to him, with hearts that know and answer to his grace.

VII.

RELIGION.

HEBREWS XII. 28.—"Let us have grace, whereby we may serve God acceptably with reverence and godly fear."

WHAT is meant by "Religion"? I do not put this question as if Religion were a strange or rarely used word. It is an extremely common word, which every one is supposed to understand. But it is used in various senses, and to most minds the term represents something very confused and vague. I propose therefore to answer the question What is Religion? as precisely as I can. I shall endeavour to shew what the most proper sense of the word is, and how it comes to be used in other senses. It is worth while for all of us to attain to clear conceptions about a term which we all have frequent occasion to use.

The following is one reason amongst others for representing to ourselves carefully what Religion is. We sometimes hear Religion put in a kind of opposition to Theology. "Let us have religion," some people say, "but not theology." If we are to agree to any such saying, we ought to know what these two things are. If you see reason to believe, as I should contend, that theology is the indispensable basis on which religion rests, you can no more give your voice for religion without theology, than you can for theology without religion. This will, I hope, be clearer to you presently.

In Holy Scripture the word Religion does not frequently occur. In the Old Testament it is not once used. We meet with it in three places of the New Testament; but in one of these there is nothing which exactly corresponds to it in the original. Let us turn to this first. It is in the Epistle to the Galatians, i. 13, 14. St Paul refers, in our translation, to his conversation in time past "in the Jews' religion," and says he had profited or advanced "in the Jews' religion" above many his equals. In the original the word rendered "the Jews' religion" is Judaism. St Paul says he had formerly lived and been forward "in Judaism." This word is like Christianity. And as we can say "the Christian religion" to mean the same thing as Christianity, so our translators used "the Jews' religion" to mean the same thing as Judaism. But when we are considering the word religion, we cannot quote this passage as containing any Scriptural illustration of it. In the other two places there is a word which is accurately rendered religion. The first is Acts xxvi. 5, where St Paul, speaking before Agrippa, happens to be saying nearly the same thing as when he speaks to the Galatians of his life and progress in Judaism. All the Jews know, he says, that after the "straitest sect of our religion I lived a Pharisee." St Paul in his youth had followed the strictest school of his country's religion, namely that of the Pharisees. The religion here referred to means the whole creed and worship of the Jews. The remaining passage is the well-known one in the Epistle of St James, i. 26: "If any man among you seem to be religious, and bridleth not his tongue, but deceiveth his own heart, this man's religion is vain. Pure religion and undefiled before God and the Father is this, to visit the fatherless and widows in their affliction, and to keep himself unspotted from the world." Here religion stands for devout habits of life. The religious man was one who had the form of godliness according to the fashion of his time. To be frequent at religious services is the most obvious and common form of religion in this sense. A man who assumes an exterior of religion, St James says, professes that he desires to worship God devoutly. Let him know that the devout worship which is real and which God approves is best shewn in charity and unworldliness.

This kind of meaning,—the habits of a devout life,—is one which the term religion may be conveniently used to express. But the most original, simple, and universal, sense of the word is *fear of God*. It denotes the awe which instinctively possesses the human mind in contemplating the supernatural. This awe or fear may be of any quality, ranging from the noblest and most exalting reverence down to the most superstitious cowardice.

An irreligious mind is a mind without this awe. With it, a people may be ignorant, cruel, fanatical, immoral, may be very far from deserving approbation; but we should not rightly characterise them as irreligious.

The religious sentiment is instinctive or natural. In no portion of humanity will you find it altogether wanting. It appears in various shapes. When driven out of one habit it will assume or create for itself another. That which is most opposite to it is thoughtlessness or superficiality of mind. If human beings can be kept in a perpetual whirl of trivial occupations and interests, the very instinct of religion may be almost starved. But wherever an atmosphere is created for it by reflection, there a feeling of awe is sure to be inspired by the mysteries of the unseen world. Religion naturally thrives where there are opportunities for solitude, and therefore for brooding. In the bustle of crowded life other influences favourable to religion come into play, such as the needs and suggestions of social and family life; but it has been generally felt by those who are engaged in incessant practical activity that occasions of retirement and spontaneous thought are necessary if the sentiment of reverence is to be kept living and fresh.

In the early stages of civilization, it has always been in a great measure through contemplating the incidents and processes of nature that the fear of the unseen powers has been developed. Man, when he is brought by contemplation face to face with nature, feels there is more at work in nature than he can understand. He perceives forces working this way and that around him which he cannot trace to their origin. These forces are the instruments of endless benefits to him; they also bring many dangers near him, and continually crush him with unforeseen but relentless strokes. Man trembles before these powers; he pays homage to beings imagined as wielding them. The more he ponders and broods, the greater is the authority which these supernatural beings exercise over his imagination. Some races of men have been more in the way of the dangerous and destructive occurrences of nature, or there has been something in their constitution or history which has led them to take more notice of these; and their religion has been more gloomy and full of fear. Others have been surrounded by the orderly and beneficent aspects of nature, or have been led to dwell chiefly on these; and their religion has been milder and more joyful. In many cases, the two elements of fear and joy have been mixed in religion so as to form very strong contrasts.

The fact that Religion has often manifested itself in hateful and cruel superstitions is an undeniable and important one, and has made this very name Religion odious in the eyes of some. Religion has been denounced as productive of evils to mankind, as unfavourable to morality. There has been an especial alliance between Religion and cruelty, illustrated by many abominable heathen rites, and by the bloody persecutions which have reddened the history of Christendom. Pious persons do not like to have the name of religion put in connexion with these horrors; they think they are bound to defend the character of Religion. But we are really not bound or concerned in any way to clear the name of Religion from these imputations. It is far better that we should honestly admit their truth; it is profitable to remember them. Understand by Religion the fear of the supernatural, the fear of what men know or imagine to be behind the veil of their ignorance; and you will not find it difficult to recognize that that fear may be either noble or base, either salutary or mischievous. In itself Religion is not to be called either bad or good; that is, it may be the one as well as the other. It is a great and important instinct of human nature, capable,—like strength, for example,—of being turned either to bad or good. It seems to me a mistake therefore to try to distinguish between Religion and Superstition,—to insist that Religion shall always mean something that we approve. It is better to bear in mind that Religion may be either a terrible curse, or an exalting and purifying and sustaining sentiment.

(2) That of which I have now spoken is the elementary and primary sense of Religion. A secondary sense in which the word is often used is that of customs and ordinances of worship. These are the forms in which religion clothes it-

self, and to these accordingly the name of religion is naturally given. We are sure that in every part of the world we shall find the fear of the unseen existing; but we do not know, till we have seen or heard, with what conceptions this fear will be associated, nor in what rites it will be expressed. The religion of one country is not the same as that of another. Temples, sacrifices, and priests to offer the sacrifices, have been the most general and striking symbols in which the spirit of religion has clothed itself. These or the like are the outward signs and witnesses of religion in a country and in the life of a people.

If any one attempts to describe a religion, he will find it impossible to keep such modes and forms of worship separate from the account of the being or beings to whom the worship is paid. So when a religion is spoken of, *the creed* and *the worship* are generally combined in one. The creed represents what is believed concerning the unseen world,—concerning God and man's relation to God. The nature of the creed always affects the nature of the worship. People fear God in a manner corresponding to what they believe concerning him. The creed, therefore, is sometimes what is chiefly meant when a religion is named. For example, when we speak of the Christian Religion, we very generally mean the system of doctrines, or the creed, supposed to be held by Christians in common.

But when it has come to mean a system of

doctrines, the word Religion has diverged considerably from its first and most proper sense. In that first sense we may call it *the fear of God.* The fear of God is expressed in various kinds of worship. Those kinds of worship are connected with, and modified by, the faith of men concerning God. So, Religion is first the fear of God; secondly, by a natural extension, the mode of worship; thirdly, the belief on which the worship is founded.

When we desire to be accurate, it is better not to use the word Religion in this third sense. There are several words we may use instead, such as creed, faith, or theology. These words denote what men hold or think concerning God. The Christian Creed or Faith or Theology denotes what we have learnt to believe concerning God through the revelation of him given to us in Christ. Our religion,—that is to say, our reverence or fear or spirit of worship,—should answer to what has been made known to us concerning God. Religion rests on Creed or Theology.

Let us dwell a little on this point. It is idle to talk of having religion without a theology. If you urge a man to be religious, he will want to know whom or what he is to regard with awe, to whom or what he is to consecrate himself. Suppose you visited a superstitious people, full of fear, given to base modes of propitiation,—how could you hope to purify their religion, to substitute, as some would say, religion for superstition? You must try to correct their theology, to lead them to a truer belief. When Barnabas and Paul were at Lystra, they found the Lycaonian people abundantly religious. Having seen a cripple enabled to walk, the people came to the conclusion that the gods had come down in the likeness of men, and they proposed to do sacrifice to them. What did Barnabas and Paul say to them, whilst they vehemently refused to be thus worshipped? "We preach to you," they said, "that ye should turn from these vanities unto the living God, which made heaven, and earth, and the sea, and all things that are therein; who in times past suffered all nations to walk in their own ways. Nevertheless he left not himself without witness, in that he did good, and gave us rain from heaven, and fruitful seasons, filling our hearts with food and gladness." Thus they sought, in teaching these heathen Lycaonians, not to make them more religious, but to give them a sounder theology, which might inspire them with a purer religion.

It was not indeed the aim of the first preachers of the Gospel anywhere to awaken in their hearers a fear of the supernatural or to make them more religious. Their commission was to tell men about God, to make announcements which had not come from man or human wisdom, but which they knew would commend themselves to the universal human conscience. They substituted a Father, revealing himself in a Son and by a Spirit, for the vanities of heathen idolatry, for the many gods of the heathen altars. With the heathen, a debasing religion had gone with a corrupt theology. They believed in gods who were capricious, selfish, immoral, revengeful; in gods who would favour the men who flattered them and gave them gifts, and would afflict those who neglected them. What good could the fear of such gods do them? Their gods were not indeed wholly evil: if they had been, the worship of them must have been wholly injurious. There was courage and generosity, grace and beauty, in the natures of the heathen gods, and so the religion of their worshippers was not without its good effects upon them. But the preachers of the Gospel declared a God who was wholly and perfectly good; a God just, loving, patient, forgiving, capable of sacrifice, desiring the highest blessedness of men his children. They proclaimed this God to men, and bade them turn away from idols, and invited them to break the spiritual bondage in which the worship of false gods held them, and enter upon the freedom which they might enjoy in serving the living God.

And, by bringing men to believe in Jesus Christ and in the Father, the preachers of Christ undoubtedly nourished in them an ever increasing fear of God. It is impossible to believe in God, to think of him, and not to fear him. The absence of a solemn religious reverence, of a fear of God, in the heart of a Christian, would have been an unnatural and incomprehensible thing to an Apostle. It is true that one of the Apostles says that perfect love casts out fear: but what does he add? " because fear hath torment." Such fear, the fear that hath torment, the fear that cripples and enslaves, does not belong to the true Christian attitude towards God. But St John would have agreed with his brother Apostles when they inculcated the fear of God. He too would have said, "Let us have grace whereby we may serve God acceptably with reverence and godly fear." He would have sympathized with that appeal of St Peter, "If ye call on the Father, who without respect of persons judges according to every man's work, pass the time of your sojourning here in fear; forasmuch as ye know that ye were redeemed from the frivolous life handed down to you from your fathers, not with corruptible things, as silver and gold, but with the precious blood of Christ."

Yes, brethren. Christians cannot but know that they have been redeemed from frivolity and levity and irreligion. A revelation has come to them which transcends all manifestations of destroying fury in its right and its power to awe the heart into reverence and fear. We shew too plainly that we do not realize what has been done for us on the part of God, if our spirits remain unimpressed by deep religious awe. Remember that God has not told us that there is no such thing as wrath, that he is a Being who may be trifled with, that if we are careless of his blessings we may at least be sure of escaping his punishments. Through all the loving life of his Son, through the sacrifice of Calvary, through the victory over hell and death, God remains a consuming fire. The terrors of the guilty are not to be cast out by irreligion, though they may be assuaged and purified by the discovery of God's forgiveness.

The key to God's character is given us in the name of *Father*. A child may be terrified by a capricious tyrant, and through the torment of this fear its whole moral nature may be crushed and distorted. But a perfectly loving and just and good parent,—if we could conceive of any earthly parent as triumphing over the weaknesses which make us such imperfect fathers and mothers,—is not a person to be regarded without reverence by a child. Such a parent has grave displeasure for offences, has stern punishment for rebellion; and the very exhibition of justice and love, apart from their functions of chastisement, is such as to inspire a susceptible human nature with reverence. So, those who best know God to be a perfect Father,—those who have most unreservedly accepted him as fully revealed in his Son Jesus Christ,—will be most thoroughly penetrated by the fear of him. Even if they did not sin, they would serve him with reverence and godly fear: but being conscious of continually sinning against God, their fear of him must be often mingled with shame and misgivings and dread.

Let us be sure, however, that true religion,—the fear of the just and gracious Father,—is a sentiment which emancipates instead of enslaving. Fear in general enslaves: when it is completely dominant it paralyzes the whole man. The fear of the true God is allied with faith and hope and love. It gives courage, instead of melting it away. To fear God is the grand remedy for all other fears. There have been many kinds of courage; it is possible for men to be brave with a gay, reckless audacity. But the courage which has stood best every kind of proof, the courage which can face the terrors of the invisible world as well as of the visible, the courage which can resist the authority of greatness and fashion, is the courage of the grave, reverent, God-fearing man, who knows that his Saviour holds the keys of death and hell. Some superstitions which have been terribly tormenting and enslaving may be dispelled, we know, by increased knowledge. Dangers supposed to lurk in the dark may be driven out by turning light upon their hiding-place. The lives of all of us are much happier than the lives of the bravest in former ages in being freed from many imaginary terrors. But I do not see how science can remove the *fear of death*,—that last crowning fear which from the beginning has held the souls of men in bondage. Faith in God is the true preservative against the fear of death which includes all other fears.

We may confidently therefore adopt the words of the Psalm, "Fear God, ye saints, and you will then Fear nothing else beside." Mere light-heartedness, the security of youth and happiness, is a graceful quality, which a thoughtful Christian need not gravely condemn. But it is not a buckler against the ills of life. Happy are they who possess, —along with that light-heartedness, if they are so constituted,—the grave convictions, the spiritual earnestness, the fear of God, in which alone true security is to be found. Let parents, if they seek the permanent well-being of their children, train them in godly fear. Let them encourage habits of reverence, habits of meditation and prayer. The young mind needs some auxiliaries in outward habits to aid it in coming face to face with God. But above all, for the young and for ourselves alike, let us keep, if we may have grace to do so, the nature and character of God clear and pure in our conceptions. Let us hallow his name, as the name of the heavenly Father, in our hearts. Let him be the Living God to us, ever present, judging according to every man's inward work, holy, just, and good. Let him be our fear, and let him be our dread. He may claim this worship at our hands: by willingly giving it to him we may inherit safety and peace.

VIII.

THE CONSCIENCE.

1 Tim. iv. 2.—"Having their conscience seared with a hot iron."

THE term Conscience, though not exclusively a Christian word, has more importance and honour in the properly Christian morality than it can have in any other. The word occurs frequently in the New Testament, and every teacher who has drunk at all deeply into the New Testament spirit has spoken of the conscience with deep interest and awe. This fact may be connected with two causes. First, the teaching of the Lord Jesus and of those who have followed him is marked by a tendency to go inwards, and not to dwell in outward actions or effects. Christian teaching is deep and penetrating. It asks at once about the affections, the heart, the will. It lays down the principle, "The evil things which come from within, out of the heart of a man, are those which defile the man:" "Cleanse first that which is within the cup and platter, that the outside of them may be clean also." The preaching of the Gospel has always been negligent of the outworks, in its zeal to gain possession of the inner citadel, the heart, out of which are the issues of life. And the conscience is that which is most inward and secret in man. Secondly, it belongs to Christian teaching to affirm emphatically a direct relation between the individual soul and God. Whenever the Gospel has had power, it has been through persuading men that they might come severally face to face with God, that God was not too infinite to have dealings with each man, that God could be offended by a man's sin, and that man's sin might be forgiven by God. The questioning of God, says the Christian teacher, "pierces even to the dividing asunder of soul and spirit and of the joints and marrow, and discerns the thoughts and intents of the heart. Neither is there any creature that is not manifest in his sight; but all things are naked and exposed unto the eyes of him with whom we have to do." The invitation to men, being thus known and judged by God, to be reconciled to him and to come into the blessedness of being his loved and trustful children, has naturally brought the conscience, with which the sense of wrongdoing and the sense of being at peace are particularly associated, into prominence. It is, in fact, upon this direct relation between God and men, between God as a Father and men as his spiritual children, that the doctrine of the conscience rests. It is in the light of that relation that the nature of what is called the conscience can be best understood. By realizing that relation we are guarded against letting the conscience become hardened, and are enabled to keep it both tender and satisfied.

It is desirable not to attribute to the conscience powers and duties which do not properly belong to it. From a desire to do honour to a faculty which holds, as I have said, so important a place in Christian teaching, people have often used exaggerated language about what the conscience does or may do. The consequences of a false estimate of the rights and powers of the conscience are first to throw the subject into confusion, and then to create a prejudice against legitimate appeals to the conscience. It has been imagined that the Creator has placed in each man's nature an infallible monitor, called by this name of Conscience, from which the man ought to take his directions,—a sort of oracle which the man may consult, and to the utterances of which he ought to yield reverent obedience. The New Testament says nothing at all to this effect, and experience certainly does not support such a theory. If the conscience is to be regarded as an infallible monitor, you will soon have two infallible monitors contradicting one another. One man's conscience will pronounce one judgment, and another man's conscience will pronounce another. The truth is, that conscience has nothing to do with forming opinions or pronouncing judgments. No one ought to speak of his conscience instructing or guiding him in any way. It is often a wise thing, when some conception has become fixed and technical, and various associations have begun to cling tightly round it, to give up for an occasion the use of the term and to endeavour to express the same thought in other language. Now when a man says that his conscience compels him to act in a particular way, he conveys the impression that some inscrutable authority to which he himself owes allegiance, but with which strangers cannot intermeddle, has spoken to him like an oracle, bidding him take this course, and leaving him no alternative. But what does he mean? If he is forbidden to use the word conscience, what will he say? He means that on the whole a certain course appears the right one for him to take. It may be really the right one. He may have taken all possible means to come to a right conclusion, and his judgment may be a sound one. But also it may not. Every man is fallible, on matters of duty as well as on other matters. On the whole we believe,—because we believe that we are made and governed by Divine wisdom,—that those who honestly desire to find and do what is right will be rightly guided. But it is impossible to affirm that any good intention will make a man infallible. Very soon, I repeat, you would have one personal infallibility set against another. A good man will have no doubt whatever, indeed, about the rightness and wrongness of many acts: but these will be those on which mankind are agreed, and on which therefore no one would think of calling in the authority of an internal oracle. On points where there is any doubt, to say, 'Some may think one thing and some another, but as for me, my conscience decides so and so,' is to set up an authority and then to bow down to it. "My conscience" should be "my judgment,"—such judgment as I, a fallible man, have been able to form. No man has any inward monitor different from the general reason and truth of things. The obligation to act according to one's conscience is simply the obligation to do what, upon the best consideration, commends itself to one as right.

Conscience says to each one, Do what is right, or *Be* right. The voice of conscience is thus unvarying, monotonous. It belongs to the judgment, or to the whole man judging as truly as he can, to find out what is right. Each man is inevitably guided in a great measure by the common sense of his time. If he does what he honestly thinks right, his conscience will acquit him. But it may happen nevertheless that the man was wrong. A higher moral standard may unequivocally condemn the conduct which a man's conscience approved. Take such simple illustrations as slave-owning, or polygamy. Where these customs were universally allowed, conscience did not protest against them. Were they then right? or, is the conscience proved to be an impostor? No; either conclusion would be wrong. The moral standard is raised gradually, through knowledge and experience. Conscience has nothing to do with forming the moral standard. It only says to each man, Be true to the best you know. And in this way it will help, it is true, in a most important degree, to advance morality.

Where slavery, for example, is being brought to an end, the most conscientious persons will admit most readily the new light, and will feel bound most unhesitatingly to make the necessary sacrifices.

There seems then to be little occasion for any man to speak about his conscience at all. If a man mentions his conscience, he generally means his opinion or conclusion, and by calling it conscience he gives a fallacious mystical authority to it. The phrase is appropriate, when there is any question of inward truthfulness or purity of motive. A man may say legitimately "In my conscience I believe so and so," or "I have nothing on my conscience," or "My conscience sustains me in what I am doing," meaning that he is inwardly true to himself and to what he believes to be right; but it is not often needful or desirable to make such a protest.

Recall to your minds what the relation of man to God is. Man is made in God's image, to know and to love God. He is under God's discipline: God is teaching him by experience and by his Spirit. Conscience denotes the feeling, the acknowledgment, that God has a claim on man. It is the confession of an ordained allegiance, on man's part, to the law and nature of God. This confession has never been entirely wanting in any portion of the human race. Where ignorance has been very great, the confession of allegiance to the Divine law has been uttered in so feeble and confused a manner that we can hardly say we recognize the action of conscience at all. But there has always been a rudimentary conscience in man. And the voice of conscience, being, as I said, monotonous, has not itself been subject to change. It has always been the simple answer, "I ought," to the Divine Voice saying, "Thou oughtest." And this is what it remains. Conscience is no oracle, no monitor or adviser. The possession of a conscience does not exempt a man in the slightest degree from the duty and necessity of getting all the knowledge he can and forming his judgment in any case according to what he knows. His conscience will not tell him whether he ought to be a Churchman or a Dissenter, a Conservative or a Liberal. It is the witness within him, springing out of the Divine constitution of his nature, that what is right has a claim upon him. It speaks against passion, against interest, against cowardice, saying continually, Be true to what is right.

I do not know that anything is gained by trying to make conscience a distinct faculty in human nature. It seems to be a Divine instinct, the instinct of allegiance, not to be eradicated without the destruction of human nature itself. As the authority which claims the allegiance,—that is, the authority of God himself,—becomes better known, the instinct of allegiance naturally gains strength. The more the whole nature of a man yields itself in obedience to the Divine government, the more will the confession of allegiance be developed. It will pervade all his thoughts and feelings, creating an instinctive repugnance to what is well understood to be displeasing to God.

The revelation of Christ brought home the Divine claims and the relationship of God to man with new and unimagined force to the hearts of men. It was natural therefore that by this revelation almost a new life should be given to the conscience. When Jesus Christ was received as the Son and image of the Eternal Maker, that natural confession of allegiance which had been evoked by the manifestations of God's order in nature and in the common government and experiences of human life, was suddenly reinforced by personal knowledge, by gratitude, by a kindling of the affections, by an inspiration of trust. The acknowledgment, "I ought," seemed cold in answer to that claim which God had put forth in Christ, the claim which God justified and commended by so transcendent a sacrifice. Conscience indeed remained the same in its own strict function: but man learnt to judge himself, as to render himself up to God, more deeply and thoroughly. God was now speaking more manifestly to the inmost spirit of a man. From the same inmost spirit the confession of allegiance was required to come, and it was found it could come. "Love so amazing, so divine, Demands my life, my soul, my all." The Christian conscience, or the human conscience in a true Christian, was the acknowledgment that the whole man when stirred to his depths belonged of right to God, as much as his external actions.

In that world of mysteries in which the relation of the soul to the invisible but ever-present God has its place, there is only the greater need of a quick and watchful conscience. In other words, a man who confesses that God has a claim upon his inward life, and that his inward life, according to God's demand, should be a life of faith and love, is in danger of self-deception. He may persuade himself, or try to persuade himself, that he is giving to God the religious service which God desires, and not an outward religious service only, but one accompanied by feeling and emotion, when he is not really giving *himself*. As a spiritual being, acknowledging God as his Father, he knows that he is bound to give *himself* to God. If he is true and watchful, he will be on his guard against this snare of giving a *portion* of himself to God and reserving himself.

Where such a watch is kept over the springs of life, there cannot but be perpetual self-condemnation; but at the same time there may be a continuous advance in moral sensitiveness, so that the whole nature of the man may instinctively protest against evil. There may be, so to speak, a tenderness of the spiritual nerve, causing it to shrink from that which is believed to be displeasing to God. This kind of shrinking is not, indeed, to be implicitly trusted. It may always serve as a valuable warning, calling for the exercise of honest conscientious judgment. But it depends to a great degree upon habit. If we have grown accustomed to think an act wrong, and afterwards are convinced that we were mistaken, a certain inward repugnance, hardly to be distinguished from the witness of the conscience, is likely to be excited for some time by the doing of the act. You may have felt how, after a painful dream, if you wake without remembering the dream, there remains a certain mental soreness which is at first unaccountable, but which explains itself when the dream is recalled. So the spiritual nature does not reconcile itself easily to an act which it has newly learnt to think of as innocent. Those who have been bred in habits of what we call puritanical strictness of Sabbath observance, if they deliberately change their opinion as to what it is expedient to do on the Sunday, may very likely not be able to write a letter or play on a musical instrument or take a walk on Sunday without feeling uncomfortable as if they were doing what is wrong. How far such feelings should be treated with deference or the contrary is a matter for thoughtful spiritual judgment and discipline. But they should never be allowed to rule, as if they were identified with the conscience. Conscience sustains deliberate judgment, rather than the feeling which depends on associations. It may be my duty to do what may positively pain my whole spiritual sensibility; and then conscience, of course, bids me do it. The bitterness of such a duty seems to find expression in that terrible saying of our Lord's, "If any man come to me, and *hate* not father and mother and wife, and brother and sister, yea and his own life also, he cannot be my disciple." No right-minded person can separate himself from those near and dear to him, without feeling *as if* he were doing wrong. But this feeling ought not to govern his conduct. Conscience says to him, Though the act may seem to you like a wicked hating of those whom you are bound to love, yet if God calls and you hear his voice, you have no alternative but to follow.

It is however this kind of diffused sensibility of the spiritual nature which we mean when we speak of a *tender* conscience; and it is the loss of it that we mean when we speak of the conscience being hardened or seared. Those who are habitually careless of inward truth gain some power to silence the voice of conscience,—a terrible power to acquire! When the Divine voice says to a man, This or that *is right*,—if he answers, I don't care what is right, I will only think what is pleasant to me, or what is to my interest,—the voice will become less and less audible to him. It may then require some rough awakening, some alarm, some unsparing humiliation, to compel him to listen again with awe to the voice of right and truth. We may harden ourselves if we choose; and, for hardening the conscience, there is nothing like that plausible worldliness which is so common a snare. You feel and see that worldliness is *hardening* where it has its own way; you can observe how the steady following of fashion makes people *callous* to all the finer spiritual appeals. If we are rightly advised, we shall be more afraid of such a self-inflicted punishment than of any chastening with which God may visit us.

Let me say a few words, before concluding, on two phrases, "a morbid conscience," "a good conscience." The first of these is used when a man is too scrupulous about small things. It is not that any one can possibly be too conscientious, too desirous of perfection. But to dwell upon little things almost certainly means to withhold due or proportionate consideration from the greater things. Those who make themselves miserable with anxiety about some action which to other sensible persons seems insignificant can hardly be giving their minds to the weightier matters, can hardly be thinking of the duty and blessedness of living on terms of free trust and affection with God. Such persons need to look higher; they need to think of God more than of themselves.

But how is it possible for any sinner, who knows himself, to have a *good* conscience? Does this mean that he is satisfied with himself? If he judges himself strictly, how can he be satisfied with himself? If he is not, what does a good conscience mean?

Let us ask, what does a *bad* conscience mean? It evidently means the condition of one who is cherishing a motive, or indulging in conduct, which he is ashamed to allow to appear. To have a good conscience is generally said with reference to other men. You may have a good conscience when you know you are not guilty of the baseness or profligacy or falsehood which might be imputed to you. From such faults as these every sinner who can claim the title of a Christian ought to be free. He may have a good conscience before his fellow-men, when he cannot reproach himself with anything which they would consider disgraceful or unworthy. But it is not the same thing to justify ourselves before God. He who gave his own Son for us, and has called us to be his children, has a different standard for us than that of men. Can we have a good conscience before God?

Only through God's *forgiveness*, and through a faith in that forgiveness. If a man does not welcome God's forgiveness, does not desire that it may cleanse him from sin, he cannot look God in the face with a good conscience. So long as he holds out against being reconciled to God, he must have a bad conscience as regards God. But if he prays for forgiveness, and accepts it, and desires to cleave to God as a gracious Father who knows the frailty of sinful humanity, then, with whatever sins and shortcomings he may have to reproach himself, these things will not separate him from God. As often as he is conscious of sin, he may call to mind the work of Christ the Son of God. He may have confidence towards God, not because he is irreproachable, but because it is the very nature and property of God always to have mercy and to forgive. The question then will come to this: Does the man turn towards God, or does he turn away from God? If he sees the face of God in Christ, and is not repelled by it but drawn towards it, he may have peace with God. He is satisfied, not with himself, but with God. This kind of satisfaction will not make him willing to remain in sin, but on the contrary anxious and earnest to be delivered from it. Yes, brethren; those who accept reconciliation with God will have both a *good* conscience, and a *tender* conscience. God grant to us this blessed and hopeful spiritual condition! may he teach us to know him as a God of purer eyes than to behold iniquity, and yet as pardoning iniquity! may he give us the confidence of the true filial heart, and at the same time the fear of displeasing him which will only increase with the growth of filial faith and love!

IX.

HUMAN CORRUPTION.

ROMANS VII. 18.—"I know that in me, that is, in my flesh, dwelleth no good thing."

THE doctrine of the general sinfulness of mankind is one which has been a great stumblingblock. How, it has been asked, can we reconcile the belief that human nature is utterly corrupt with that trust in human nature and with that hope for the progress of society which all kindly and well-disposed persons desire to cherish? To hold that the world is utterly wicked, and to look for a coming of Christ to overwhelm it with vengeance, may be orthodox; but can this be the way of thinking of those who desire to take a cheerful part in increasing the virtues and correcting the evils of society?

It is evident beyond dispute that in the Bible and in all theology which has ever taken hold of the conscience the sinfulness of universal human nature is strongly affirmed. Where the theological feeling has been intense, there the corruption, the depravity, of human nature has been described with great energy of language. To minds dwelling on the perfections and the claims of God, and desiring to pay the utmost possible homage to God, it has seemed obvious to call the nature of man altogether vile and miserable and evil. The best and holiest of men,—all with the one exception of Jesus Christ,—have spoken of themselves with shame and even with loathing; and what could be said against *them* could obviously be said with more truth against men of inferior quality. In all earnest sermons therefore, in the hymns which express the more fervid emotions of the soul, in the doctrinal formularies of stern and thoroughgoing minds, the essential sinfulness of human nature is prominently set forth. More indulgent and liberal views of human nature are felt for the most part by deeply religious persons to belong to a less theological atmosphere,—to be natural, that is, to those who start from the world and not from God, who make the common opinions and capabilities of men and not the perfections and claims of God the ruling objects of their contemplations, and whose estimate of human life is therefore on the whole superficial.

Now this strongly felt corruption of human nature, when it is taken out of its right place and proper relations, may become a monstrous and unnatural figment. It is liable to be abused by those who frame and support systems of theology, to be misunderstood and misrepresented by those who repudiate theology.

The corruption of human nature is abused by those who believe in it when they make it the first and fundamental article of the Christian faith. It does not belong, properly speaking, to revelation. It is a fact, a character, which is assumed and brought out by revelation; but the things revealed, the foundations and proper objects of our faith, are the righteousness and love and forgiveness of God. These are what every confession of faith ought to aim at setting forth, and not the faults and imperfections of man.

As I believe, therefore, there has been great misjudgment on the part of theologians and religious schools in drawing out the depravity of human nature from its relative and dependent place, and making it an absolute and primary object of faith. This course has given excuse to unbelievers for fastening upon this as the characteristic tenet of Christian theology. But, apart from such perversion, I have no doubt that the eye of unbelievers would have been caught by the strong affirmations of human sinfulness occurring in what I hold to be their legitimate place,—in the complaints of the prophets, in the profound theological expositions of St Paul, in the fervid utterances of repentance and adoration. It is too natural to be wondered at that they should say, 'What an unreal doctrine this is! Who really believes that every human being is utterly wicked? These people who call themselves miserable sinners are in fact and know themselves to be a very good sort of people. They are for the most part honest, humane, and conscientious. What a tottering structure must the Christian faith be, when it rests upon such an unbelieved figment as this of universal depravity!'

With reference to comments like these, let me ask your attention to two considerations:—

1. The corruptness of human nature, as it appears in Scripture and in such theology as agrees best with Scripture, professes to be simply a fact of experience and observation, liable to be tested and corrected by the same processes by which it is found out. Good men have spoken of themselves as mysteriously and perversely inclined to evil. Why?—Not because they were bound to do so by any creed, but because they were conscious of it. I suppose they knew what they felt. In the Old Testament, such language as "Behold, I was shapen in wickedness, and in sin hath my mother conceived me" is a confession of King David, whom no one thinks of as the worst of men, whom, in spite of his flagrant faults, we are accustomed to regard with veneration. In the New Testament, the corresponding language is chiefly St Paul's. He says, "I am carnal, sold under sin.... The good that I would I do not: but the evil which I would not, that I do." St Paul was a man, so far as we know, of singular blamelessness as well as of pre-eminent self-devotion. Now, there is no reason whatever to suppose that either of these men had been taught that it was the right thing to confess himself to be a miserable sinner. There was no such dogma in the creed of the Jews: there was no such dogma in the Gospel as Saul of Tarsus had received it. The faith of King David was in the righteousness of Jehovah; the faith of St Paul was

that the same Jehovah, the God of his fathers, had sent his Son to be the Saviour of the world. Those confessions of sinfulness were the sincere and spontaneous utterances of what they felt.

These same men and others, looking abroad on the world, said very strong things of the evil tendencies and evil acts of their countrymen and the surrounding nations. One, for example, has left the words, " Corrupt are they, and become abominable in their wickedness, there is none that doeth good." Why did they say such things? Were they speaking conventionally, in deference to the exigencies of their creed? No: in the first place their words bear the stamp of personal feeling; and in the next place, there is no sign of their having had any creed which required them so to speak. They deplored the wickedness of mankind because they saw it. They had no other reason for regarding men as inclined to evil, except the lamentable fact, as it appeared to them, that they were so.

No more have we. If all that has been changed, we are not bound to speak of human nature as worse than we find it.

But it is important to understand how it was that these men of the Bible came to have such strong impressions. They had their eyes fixed upon the perfect goodness of God. It was their faith that there was a living God in heaven, not merely distant in unapproachable purity, but mixing himself with men his creatures and children, making his qualities known to them, inviting them to look to him, and enabling them through that worship and trust to become like him. The Apostles of Jesus Christ were continually living in the presence and fellowship of One in whom the glory of the Divine nature had shone as the glory of perfect sonship and perfect brotherhood. They felt themselves claimed by a transcendent sacrifice to be true in thought and word and deed to their Master and to the Father. In the light of Divine glory therefore they judged of human shortcomings. When do you perceive anything to be soiled? Is it when all the things that surround it are in the same condition, and under a dim light? Or, when it is contrasted, in broad daylight, with something else that is spotlessly white? The glory of God in the face of Jesus Christ, shining into human hearts, made many things seem defiled and unworthy which before had passed muster well enough.

The corruption of human nature, then, is treated in Scripture and is to be regarded by us as a fact of experience, subject to any of the corrections of experience.

II. But there is a second consideration, of at least equal importance. All Scriptural theology invariably recognizes in human nature more than a merely human element. We have just now heard the penitent David charging himself with being utterly sinful: "Behold, I was shapen in wickedness, and in sin hath my mother conceived me." But what does he go on to say? "Thou shalt purge me with hyssop, and I shall be clean; thou shalt wash me, and I shall be whiter than snow.... Make me a clean heart, O God, and renew a right spirit within me. Cast me not away from thy presence, and take not thy holy Spirit from me. O give me the comfort of thy help again, and stablish me with thy free Spirit." This shame-stricken sinner had before enjoyed the comfort of God's help, and hoped to enjoy it again. He had fallen in a way which made him feel that there was an evil tendency at the very heart of his being; but the man David, as he lived amongst his fellow-men and was known to them, was not a merely evil creature. The Spirit of God upheld him, when by himself he would have fallen to the ground. There was a better nature in him, given from above, as well as that evil nature which mastered him when he sank in self. St Paul, again, our New Testament example, claims the better as well as the worse nature. He does not know which to call *himself*. He is conscious of two dispositions struggling against one another within him, and of either of them he may say, "*I* desire this, *I* desire that." When the rebellious disposition is urging him to act, his conscience protests against it, and he feels that he may say, "It is no more *I* that do it, but sin that dwelleth in me." But in the very next words he adds, "For I know that in *me* (that is, in my flesh) dwelleth no good thing." He could not help saying, "*I* lust, *I* rebel;" and at the same time, "*I* know better, I consent unto the law that it is good." "So then," he concludes, "with the mind I myself serve the law of God, but with the flesh the law of sin." Inwardly, St Paul was conscious of this struggle, the best explanation of which he found in referring all that was good in him to God, and all that was evil to self separated from God. Outwardly, he appeared to his fellow-men anything but a bad, corrupt creature; he appeared to them noble and admirable. Nor would he have said in his humblest moments that they were wrong in thinking well of him. Only he bade them refer what was good in him to the grace of God. "Not I, but the grace of God which was in me."

You will understand that when once this doctrine of God working in the souls of men and changing and sustaining their dispositions is admitted, the conception of a universal human corruption is greatly modified. Each man becomes as it were two men. There is the old man going to decay according to the deceitful lusts, but there may be also the new man created after the Divine likeness in true righteousness and holiness. All the strong language concerning the essential sinfulness of human nature will apply to the old man, to the man as he is in the flesh, to the man as he is in self. It will leave untouched the new man, the man as he is in the spirit, the man as he lives by faith in a higher and a better. And you will find that the religious persons who have spoken, as it may have seemed, most extravagantly of the depth and universality of sinfulness have always been those who have been most possessed by the belief that God deserts no man, but is close to each,—that in God we live and move and are.

III. If then the question is raised, What is on the whole the prevalent character of the human race, or of any people or society?—such a believer as St Paul is in no way hampered by any religious theory about original corruption in endeavouring to give a true and fair answer. He may very possibly have a more favourable opinion of mankind than some cynical person who holds that every one is born good, but is afterwards spoilt, more or less, by bad laws and customs. If he believes in Divine inspiration, he will *prefer* thinking as well of men as he can, because he will then be recognizing a more fruitful activity of that inspiration. It must always pain a Christian to think that human sinfulness can oppose such a resistance as it does to the good Spirit of God.

But the question whether there is more good or evil in mankind generally is not a very useful one to raise, because the answer to it must depend entirely on the standard by which character is to be measured. A kindly-disposed person, assuming a sort of easy average of morality, may form a very favourable judgment of mankind. Fix the standard higher, and the human nature of this age does not pass so well. Theology, or the habit of referring all things to God, tends to raise the standard of judgment. It keeps or ought to keep before the mind the ideal of a true child of God, of a true family of God; and surely, judged by this ideal, the best man and the best community must seem to come lamentably short. On the other hand it accustoms us to believe that God is moving where we do not see him, and so to hope the best continually. But it makes no attempt to strike the balance between the amount of evil and the amount of good in the world. Good and evil are in the eyes of a Christian believer too spiritual, too personal, too mysterious, to be fit subjects for that kind of ponderation. Such a man says rather of himself, "In me, that is in my flesh, dwells no good thing. There is no health in us. But I know also that the grace of God is sufficient for me and for all, and that his strength is made perfect in weakness."

It may possibly occur to some one to think, "Then this old Scriptural doctrine of universal sinfulness is explained away. Taken in a straightforward sense it says that every one is extremely wicked. You protest it does not mean that. Then you make it mean nothing." I reply that, though, as I believe, it pronounces no judgment whatever upon the actual goodness or badness of an individual or of a society, it is yet a doctrine, or to speak more accurately, an experience, which cannot be absent from an earnest Christian faith and a sincere Christian life. The contemplation of the Divine goodness, the acknowledgment of God's fatherly claim upon us, the acceptance of Christ's life and spirit as our true standard, will inevitably bring out the sense of sin as something deadly, haunting, indestructible, sitting close to the springs of our personal being. I do not hold that sin is trivial because I see that it is not overwhelmingly dominant. I recognize sin as exceeding sinful, and the righteousness of God as striving against it and subduing it.

Let me put what I have been endeavouring to say, dear brethren, in the form of two practical conclusions.

(1) If we desire to be uncompromising Christians, Scriptural old-fashioned Christians, there is no reason why we should not take as charitable a view of the motives and character of our neighbours as the facts will allow us to take. Why, to be Christian is to be charitable; and it is one of the signs of charity that it "hopeth all things." Don't give up the deep serious feeling about sin as an instinct of rebellion against the law of God from which no human soul is to be supposed to be exempt. But keep that feeling in its place by believing in the grace of God as visiting all human souls, soliciting, guarding, inspiring them.

You look upon young children;—the more you have of the Spirit of Jesus Christ in you, the more you feel inclined to rejoice in them, to bless them, to think well of them. Does some perversion of your creed whisper in you, But ought I not to think of these as beings wholly corrupt,—at least until I can discern proofs of a complete change of nature? Answer, that no doctrine of Christ ever taught us to call good evil, although Christ and his followers have always taught us to refer all good to God,—not to man in himself, but to God working with man. Say then, So far, indeed, as these are mere children of the flesh, there is no good in them. But to me they are children of God; and I rejoice to see that there is a great deal of good in them, which confirms me in my belief.

Let me remind you how our Church, in its office for that very Sacrament which embodies the idea of a natural corruption and defilement, speaks of the ordinary human nature of children. After reciting the Gospel story which tells us how Jesus welcomed some little children,—not some select children, but chance specimens of the Jewish children of the day,—the minister is bidden to say, "Ye hear in this Gospel the words of our Saviour Christ, that he commanded the children to be brought unto him,—how he blamed those that would have kept them from him; how he exhorteth all men to follow their innocency." And because Christ loved and blessed the innocence of little children, therefore we are encouraged to have confidence in bringing our little innocent children to our heavenly Father's baptism. It is striking that in the administration of this Sacrament of cleansing, the children, *before their Baptism*, should be so explicitly declared to be loveable and innocent in the sight of God and of Christ.

If we Christians then are to differ from men of

the world and unbelievers in judging of men in general, let it not be ours to be more suspicious, more harsh, less ready to ascribe good motives. Let us without misgivings assume our neighbours to be good till we are compelled by proof to think them bad. The world knows as well as we do, that there is no danger of any mortal brother overthrowing our theology by shewing himself pure from every taint of evil.

(2) But again, while we are not only at liberty, but are bound, to judge others in this favourable spirit, it is certain that as we grow in spirituality we shall see more truth and reality in the old lamentations over the clinging sinfulness of the human heart. You must have had some perception of this yourselves. The Christians who have gone before us cannot have deceived us when they have testified with one voice that along with the knowledge of God and of his Son Jesus Christ grows the knowledge of the deep infection of our nature. Try to conquer a disposition of which your conscience accuses you, try to cast out the roots of some sin from your hearts; think how unworthy it is of you, how displeasing it must be to the Spirit of God: do you succeed at once or altogether in your attempt? What is it hinders you? Aim at a higher and more Christian tone of life; seek to be more trustful, more full of joy and hope, more tolerant of annoyances, more pure and heavenly-minded, more courageous against the authority of the world and the threatenings of evil,

more sympathizing with the unattractive, more forgetful of self:—do you find a difficulty in realizing such an aim? Why should you? How can you reflect on your failures without groaning over the tenacity of the sin which lives in our members? Surely we have good reason not to be self-complacent or self-righteous. We have reason to condemn ourselves sincerely, and to pray for forgiveness. We have reason to give ourselves up with the whole effort of faith into God's hands, that he may drive out our sin with his righteousness, and make us through willing submission to his love the obedient instruments of his purpose.

X.

HUMAN HOLINESS.

1 CORINTHIANS I. 2.—"Called to be saints."

WE do not now use the word *saints* as St Paul and his fellow-labourers were accustomed to use it. When we read in the New Testament of "*the saints*" in this place or in that, what does the term stand for? The saints, as we easily see, are all the members of the Church of Christ, whatever their personal character may be, good, bad, or indifferent; they are all *the Christians* in the place. The word, in fact, which we should use where St Paul uses "saints" is this word "Christians." If a missionary at the present day were to address a letter to those who had received the Gospel in a heathen city, he would very likely describe them as all the Christians there, and he would by no means be understood as implying that there were no questionable believers amongst them; but he would hardly call them "the saints." It is not natural to us, and hardly anything could make it natural, to apply the title "saints" to a promiscuous body of professing Christians. I, for example, could not, without feeling that I was using something like a foreign language, speak of ourselves here now as the saints gathered together for worship within these walls. But that was the way in which the word was used in New Testament times.

To us the word "saint" almost inevitably suggests a life apart from the common work of the world. We apply this title, above all, to those who have been delivered by death from the bonds and defilements of the flesh,—the spirits of just men made perfect. We apply it also to those who have lived in other ages, especially in the primitive Christian ages, persons whom we think of almost exclusively in connexion with their religious life or their sufferings, not as men and women having their work in the world to do. In very rare cases we speak of Christians of our own time as saints, and call their lives saintly; but it is almost always a particular type of character that is thus designated. Our saints are women rather than men, persons who by ill-health or other cause have been kept out of the common tasks and the common enjoyments of human life, rather than those who have roughed it with their fellows.

It is convenient perhaps that there should be a word to designate this particular type of character. We know pretty well what we mean when we describe a life as a saintly one. We know that we could hardly use this epithet to describe the goodness,—however perfect the goodness might be,—say of a general in command of an army, or of an active and vigorous politician, or of a thriving tradesman. But it is a great price to pay for this special use of the word "saints" and "saintliness," that we are thrown out of gear, as it were, in reading the same words in the Bible. When you remember that "holy" is the English form of "saint" and has precisely the same meaning, you will realize at once the great place which the idea of holiness or saintship occupies in the thoughts of the sacred writers. Whether you look in the Old or in the New Testament, you find the term equally prominent. And you perceive these differences between the modern and the Biblical use of the term,—that whilst with us it is applied to rare and exceptional individuals, in the Bible it is applied to the general body; whilst with us it denotes a feminine, in the Bible it rather denotes a masculine, type of character; whilst with us it is associated with seclusion and meditation, in the Bible it is associated with action and the rough work of the world.

In the Old Testament, holiness is the most distinguishing character of the people whose sacred books constitute that volume. The children of Israel are called a holy people. Now the Israelites were not by any means, to judge from their own books, a race of a peculiarly gentle and fastidious disposition. They were a stiffnecked people. They were somewhat fierce, given to complaining and rebellion, desperate fighters, often cruel and brutal. They were all this, whilst at the same time they were distinguished by the rarest and noblest qualities. It is this stern and tough race of men, a people of tumultuous and bloody annals, that is throughout designated a holy people. They were continually reminded by their priests and prophets that they were holy. Their institutions, especially those which were most peculiar, were intended to convey the same assurance and the same witness. Their life was made burdensome by regulations and distinctions, concerning holy and unholy, clean and unclean things, which had the purpose of stamping the idea of holiness into their minds. As we read this morning, "I gave them my sabbaths"—why?—"to be a sign between me and them, that they might know that I am the Lord that *sanctify* them." We never find it said or implied that there were a few Israelites, the pious and unworldly ones, that were holy. It is always the people, the whole seed of Abraham, that is holy.

When the preachers of Christ, whose words are recorded in the New Testament, came to speak of holiness, they were simply carrying on the old language of their religion. It was not a newly invented term to describe something peculiarly Christian. But they no doubt gave the word "holy" a somewhat different application. Before Christ came, the Jews were holy, the Gentiles were not holy. In Christ, the dividing-fence between Jew and Gentile was seen to have been taken away. But it is still a body, a multitude, that is called holy. The holy, the saints, in the New Testament, are not the few who were distinguished by devotion and unworldliness. They are the body of baptized men, all professing Christians, amongst whom there were many, as we know, who brought great reproach upon their name. These however with the rest formed the society collectively described as the saints.

Therefore holiness, in the Bible sense, did not consist in the dispositions of the individual soul. It was not a greater predominance of religious habits which entitled any one to be called a saint.

In what, then, *did* the holiness consist? The true answer is given in the phrase I took for my text. The holiness consisted in the *calling*, "called to be saints."

It was this that made the children of Israel a holy people. Jehovah their God had *called* them. They dated their origin from the Call of their father Abraham. God had called him; he had obeyed the call, and followed the Divine hand. God made a covenant with him, and included his seed with him in the covenant. "I will be your God, and you shall be my people; and in you shall all the nations of the earth be blessed." This then was the meaning of that holiness of which we read so much in the Old Testament. The Jewish nation was holy, because it was in covenant with God, because it belonged to God. It was a *called* or *chosen* nation, and in this sense it was a *holy* nation.

Under the New Covenant, the holiness consisted in a precisely similar manner in the calling, but the call was not the same. *Now*, the promise was not to Jews and to their children only, but also to all that were afar off. The Son of Man was proclaimed as Lord and Saviour, and all the ends of the earth were invited to look to him and to be saved. The Gospel was preached to the Jew first, and also to the Gentile. In Christ Jesus there was neither Jew nor Greek, barbarian, Scythian, bond or free. Those who accepted the call received a baptism or washing, in token of the putting away of their sins. They were thus marked as members of the called society. God himself, they believed, had called them into the fellowship of his Son Jesus Christ. In this sense and for this reason they were holy or saints. The society of believers in Christ belonged to God; it was admitted into a filial relation towards God; it was breathed upon by the Spirit of God: all therefore who had been taken into this society were bound to regard themselves as holy.

Everywhere throughout the New Testament you may recognize that the holiness of Christians is thus grounded upon the Divine calling. The natural feeling of the Christian teachers on this matter is uttered in such addresses as this: "Holy brethren, partakers of the heavenly calling." Why were the brethren holy? Because they were partakers of the heavenly calling. A single Christian was not so much *a* saint, as one of *the saints*. He shared in the holiness which was common to him with his brethren. All who had heard the call of God in the Gospel were claimed to be God's family and to know him in filial love. In virtue of this Divine election they were all holy.

It is true that we find passages in which the Christians are not only told that they *are* holy, but are exhorted *to be* holy. "As he which has called you is holy, so be ye holy in all manner of conversation ; because it is written, Be ye holy, for I am holy." This kind of language belongs to the whole mystery of man's condition and duty. It assumes that we are *to be*, by voluntary conformity, that which God has first made us. God has made us his children ; therefore we are to be his children : God has made us holy to himself ; therefore we are to be holy to him : God has called us ; therefore we are to be loyal to our calling : God has redeemed us from bondage ; therefore we are to live as free men : God has reconciled us to himself ; therefore we are to be at peace and in harmony with God. Language of this kind is peculiarly characteristic of Christian teaching. Logically, it is difficult to give the full sense to either member of these statements without excluding the other. You might say, 'If God has done all, what remains for us to do?' Or, 'If we are to do all, what is there that God has done?' For example, it might be argued, 'If God has made us holy, then we *are* holy, and there is an end of it ; it is a contradiction to exhort us to be holy, as if it were possible for us to be otherwise.' Or, 'If we are to use our best efforts to *become* holy, then we must not assume that we are already holy ; it is a contradiction to talk of God having made us holy.' But in practice, in the deeper spiritual life, this contradiction does not present itself to trouble us. There is no ground for moral action so secure, no help so great, as the faith and knowledge that God has made us what we ought to be. And amongst the Christian teachers of all ages, you will find that those whose own experience has been deepest and most intense, and who have most powerfully moved others, have been those who have been inclined to lay the most stress on God's call and God's work. Such were St Paul, St Augustine, Luther,—to mention only some of the greatest. These men have discovered the helplessness of the human will, when it starts from itself; and they have learned how that will may be guided and strengthened when it aims at nothing but to rest upon and conform to and carry out the Divine will.

Those then who by God's calling *are* saints should find in the faith of this calling the true reason and strength for *being* saints. They should say to themselves, 'In God's gracious purpose, and by his explicit call, we are holy; let us take care not to defile this holiness by anything profane.'

Now, brethren, if we were to apply to our condition and duty these Scriptural ways of thinking about holiness, we should be guarded from any artificial conceptions of what saints are, and should seek to learn the nature of that sanctity of which we all are or should be partakers, by considering what our *calling* is, with which God has called us.—

But are we called? we all who are present here? Surely we are. The very least that the most lightly-worn Christian profession can signify implies a certain Divine calling. We receive the Gospel—that is, God's message of forgiveness and reconciliation through his Son. Our fathers received it before us, and through them it came down to us. We are, let us admit, hereditary Christians, Christians by transmission. But still in this way the Gospel *has* come down to us; we have received it, and that is God's call. In token of our having received this call, we have been made partakers of that one Baptism which is for the remission of sins, that Baptism which is the outward and traditional witness and organ of God's reconciliation. We have been christened; we are Christians; in Bible language we are holy to the Lord, we are of "the saints."

Let me dwell a moment on this name of Christians, because as I have said it is our modern substitute for the Scriptural word saints. Those who would not think of calling the mass of us holy would not refuse us the title of Christians. And we, brethren, would not give up this name. Conscious as we may be of our unworthiness, we yet, as baptized men and members of the great universal Christian society, call ourselves and desire to be called by the Christian name. Well, then, to you it may be said, "Christian brethren, men and women whom God by his Providence and call has made Christians, *be* Christians; be true genuine

Christians." And if you want to know what it is to be Christians, the way, the only safe way, is to inquire what is your calling. You will not, if you are wise, seek to collect from traditional religious opinion what peculiarities make up the Christian character. You will ask, rather, "To what has God called us? What has he made us?" And you will conclude that this is what it is right and necessary for us to be.

By seeking to be Christians according to God's purpose and calling, and not according to any traditional idea of the Christian character, we shall be seeking just that kind of Christianity, that kind of holiness, which will fit in with the circumstances and occupations of each. You may find excuses for not being religious in this way or in that; you may satisfy yourselves that you have no calling to saintship,—to Protestant saintship any more than to that which is admired in the Roman Church. But what can you say as to the kind of life *to which your Maker calls you?* have you no calling to that? What can you say as to an appropriate Christian life? will you plead that you have no calling to that? Think then what the Christian society is, and what it must mean to be members of it. Allow for circumstances; make the most of difficulties; give yourselves every possible indulgence. Say, for example, 'I have to work hard, and have no time to think about these things.' Or 'I am beset by difficulties when I think about them, and can by no means see my way clearly.'

Or 'I am no scholar, and cannot read the good books which the religious read.' But then ask, 'For me, set where I am, what does it mean to be a Christian? If God has called me to be a Christian, what ought I in my circumstances to be?'—Your Maker, it is certain, does not require or mean you to be anything that you can't be. But if he has called you to be at peace with him through repentance and faith, is that impossible for one in your position? If God has called you to commit yourself and those dear to you into his Fatherly keeping, can you plead that that is not in your line? If he has shewn you the privilege of being unselfish and kind, can you reject this privilege as unsuited to you? If he has forbidden you to indulge your appetites to excess or irregularly, to give way to bad tempers, to cherish prejudices, because these acts are contrary to the nature of his children, will you say you are *not* his children and therefore may freely do these things? If he has shewn you his own image in our Lord Jesus Christ his Son, and has called you to follow him, in truthfulness, in courage, in self-devotion, in love,—what will you say? I am too busy or too ignorant or too perplexed, to be truthful, to be courageous, to be self-denying, to be considerate of others?—No, brethren: you can find no bar or prescription against your true *calling*. What God in his creative purpose makes you, *that* you ought to be, whatever the cost, whatever the circumstances. You cannot escape from this exhortation; you that are

Christians, sons of the Gospel, *be* Christians! You may not profess to be religious, to be saints: well, then, be what you profess to be; decline to be what your conscience sustains you in not professing to be; but if you are Christians, be Christians.

We all know, really, how much is involved in that calling. Nothing, surely, but self-accusation, self-condemnation, is possible for us, when we once begin to judge ourselves in sincerity. We have reason to cry, May God forgive us! may God help us! We must confess that we have been too careless of the grace with which he has blessed us, of the privileges to which he has called us.

I have been afraid that we should not recognize so universally the exhortation which speaks to us as saints, and bids us live as those who are called to be saints. But there is a force and simplicity in the right idea of *holiness*, which it is indeed a pity to lose. Holiness implies separation to God from whatever is unworthy of God's presence;—not separation from work, from politics, from trade, from recreation, because these are not displeasing to God, but separation from the evil thoughts and acts which offend him. To say, Be ye holy, for God is holy, is to say, Guard your God-given soul from ill-will, from lust, from idleness, from whatever your conscience feels to be profane. There is a lofty perfection and purity in the Divine holiness which ought to be and may be our constant *aim*, though we shall be very far from reaching it. And if we could see souls as God sees them, depend upon it, we should not find that the most active are the least holy. Every state of life has its own temptations, its own difficulties; but over all states the grace of God broods, and into all the misery of our human sinfulness enters to corrupt and to enfeeble. He will be in truth the holiest, who least attempts to build up any holiness of his own, and who consents with the most simplicity to be just what God would have him be and what God by his Spirit will make him.

XI.

LIVES OF THE SAINTS.

HEBREWS VI. 12.—"Be not slothful, but followers of them who through faith and patience inherit the promises."

To-day, as you are aware, is called in our Calendar All Saints' Day. It has the distinction of a special Collect, Epistle, and Gospel, in the Prayer-book. There are not a great number of days thus distinguished. I find on counting that in addition to those which commemorate events in the life of our Lord, there are sixteen which bear the names of leading persons in the history of the Gospel, as Apostles and Evangelists, and two others, one that of Michael and All Angels, the other this of All Saints. It was a part of the work of our Church at the Reformation to reduce the number of persons thus honoured by special commemoration. A good many other names are barely retained in the Calendar, but it was thought expedient to admit into the Prayer-book services only those which were eminent, as I have described, in New Testament history. There were good reasons, no doubt, for this judgment. It disposes at once of many difficult questions as to the comparative claims of persons who are to be recognized by name in the general worship of the Church. But the arguments are certainly not all on one side. It is not desirable that we should be led to think that New Testament names are alone worthy to be cherished with affectionate veneration by Christians. There are eminent Christians of subsequent ages who may be remembered by us with more advantage than St Simon or St Jude. It would be a real gain to us, if we could have a selection made by some infallible authority of the best men to be remembered by us, taken not only from the first century, but from the second and the third and so on down to the nineteenth. Our Church has not ventured on this attempt. What it has done is this: It sanctions and commends to us the principle of cherishing personal memories and studying personal examples in the Church by choosing names taken from a field limited in itself and regarded by the whole Church Catholic as exceptional,—I mean that of the New Testament history; and then it further bids us keep one day at the end of our list of saints' days, as the day of all saints,—thus reminding us that St Andrew and St Peter and St Paul and the rest are not the only saints, but that we have a vast heritage of examples which we are obliged thus to crowd together because they are so many and because we do not know how to distinguish amongst them.

"All Saints," then, are the great cloud of witnesses by whom we find ourselves compassed about when we move backwards in thought through the ages of church history. To remember those who have gone before us, who have trodden to the end the path we are treading, who have fought in the honourable conflict in which we also are fighters, seems a kind of spiritual obligation; but it is also one of the best exercises for spiritual training. The lives of the saints are always in some form a chief part of the spiritual food of every generation. There is nothing that influences most of us so much as the contemplation of what other men, men whom we revere, have done and believed and suffered. Being dead, the saints yet speak to us. Their experiences are assimilated by us and enter into our own lives. The pious propagate their piety; the brave man propagates his courage: there is a spiritual descent and inheritance more sure than that of race.

Look at the Bible, the universal book of the Christian church. It consists in great part of lives and acts. All its other teaching is impressed with the stamp of personality. The real interest of the Scriptural books centres about persons, who reproduce and exhibit in their human lives the purposes of the Father of all. On no other plan could the Bible have been to so great an extent the common book of children and of philosophers. A human being, simple and true, bearing a part in a great Divine development, is a treasure of knowledge to all. The crown of all that the Bible has to reveal to us is the life of the Son of God in our flesh; no one can fail to learn something from that, hardly any one has even imagined that he has penetrated to the depths of it, and exhausted all that it has to teach.

And in every age of the church those who have been interested in promoting a true religious spirit have felt that there is no study so natural, so attractive, so powerful, as that of the lives of good men. There has been no difference in this respect between Roman Catholics and Protestants. All sects and schools have had their lives of the saints. The Protestant has not so interpreted his formula "the Bible and the Bible alone," as to exclude from his study the lives of those who have consecrated his principles by their godliness and their endurance. No doubt much exclusiveness has been shewn in the selection of saints to be honoured. There have been favourite Catholic saints and Protestant saints, Church saints and Nonconformist saints. Some choice in this respect in not only natural but reasonable. Let the name of All Saints however be a witness to us against narrowness and bigotry. Let us not take for granted that loyalty to God and to Christ is to be measured exactly by agreement with our own opinions. Let us have courage to admire those who have differed from us. And let it be a pride and an encouragement to us to contemplate the innumerable company, the splendid cloud, of those who tell us that there is a God in whom men may safely trust, a Saviour who leads and supports those who follow him; that this world is a part and subject of an invisible kingdom, and that they do well who live not for the seen but for the unseen.

I spoke recently of the difficulty which we find in recovering the Scriptural sense of the word *saints*. The word to our ears suggests separation from the business of the world rather than vigorous work in the world. In the New Testament, as I shewed, "the saints" are all the members of the Church, all whom we should call *Christians;* and their sanctity or holiness was regarded as depending not on their personal character but on their calling. The ecclesiastical use of the word with which we are now concerned is not precisely the same as this. The saints whom we are encouraged specially to remember are certainly those whose personal character was such as to entitle them to remembrance. But we must still be on our guard against such an idea of saints as that which associates them with the cloister or the sick room rather than with the work of the world. They were a rough kind of saints, fierce rather than gentle, who are referred to in the second lesson for this morning, Gideon, and Barak, and Samson, and Jephthah, David also, and Samuel and the prophets. If we were to seek a few words to characterize the saints whom we ought to follow, we could not find better than those which our text supplies. They were men of *faith*, and of *patience*. By faith they overcame the world; by patience they stood fast under the trials of their conflict. Whatever their opinions may have been, whatever their imperfections and lapses even may have been, men of eminent faith and of eminent patience are witnesses of the best things to us and worthy leaders in the onward march of humanity.

Such men have been the living heart of the Church, the salt of the earth. I need not say that they have not always been honoured and promoted in their lifetime. It is one of the most wholesome lessons of their lives to us, that the approval of the world does not always reward those who most faithfully serve God and mankind. Of many such might the world say, "This was he, whom we had sometimes in derision, and a proverb of reproach: we fools accounted his life madness, and his end to be without honour: how is he numbered among the children of God, and his lot is among the saints!" The true saints have encountered difficulties which were mountains requiring all their faith to remove; they have undergone tribulations, such as neglect, persecution, contempt, which proved their Divine gift of patience to the utmost.

In the Church of Christ, and outside also of the nominal Church of Christ, when we have the opportunity of becoming acquainted with the history of any generation, we see how the number of witnesses for God is continually being swelled by men of faith and patience; and their multitude is impressive through its very indefiniteness. But it is a suitable thing, and plainly intended by the Providence of God, that we should try to obtain a closer acquaintance with the good Christians who have been in some way nearer to ourselves, with those for example of our own race and country, whose circumstances and trials and achievements we may be better able to understand. Lives of worthy Englishmen are precious treasures to us and to our children. There is a continuous national life which is enriched by every faithful life that is thrown into it, and the contribution is the more valuable when such a life is made the subject of an interesting record. It is far from being true, indeed, that the lives which are most written about are always the noblest. We may believe without regret—rather with thankfulness—that there are many high examples of faith and patience which are hardly known except to God. In order to serve for the instruction of many, a life must not only have been intrinsically a noble one,—it must have been passed in the midst of interesting circumstances, such as the hard-fought conflict of a good cause; and it must not be without another advantage, that of being well and livingly set forth.

It has done good to many, and it will do good to many more, to contemplate a life thus set on high for our admiration, which has not yet passed out of the memory of contemporaries,—the pure and sweet and high-toned life of William Wilberforce. It is to a great cause, the war against slavery, that Wilberforce owes his distinction. Not being one of the greatest of men, nor one of the most severely tried, he was a man who for his resistance to the temptations of his class, for his kindliness and innocence, for his persevering devotion to a generous cause through the seductions of a comfortable English life, and for his sincere and reverent piety, is well worthy to be one of our later saints. Our kinsmen across the Atlantic had to finish their war against slavery in a far more terrific struggle than any through which we in ours had to pass,—a struggle of which the passions and animosities still confuse the characters of those engaged in it. But with them the crisis of this struggle will be associated with the memory of a man made of rougher and sterner stuff than our philanthropist, a man of genuine faith and patience, a steadfast God-fearing ruler; and Americans, according to the testimony of those who know best, will have good cause to revere the memory of Abraham Lincoln as one of the faithful men whom it will be their privilege and their glory to follow.

The history of the Hebrew people is one of continual wars, and there is scarcely one of the Old Testament saints who is not associated with fighting. We have happily fallen upon more peaceful times. But there is still something in the soldier's calling which exercises and sets off to peculiar advantage a simple and manly piety. I suppose there is no religious biography which has been more popular in our time than that of Hedley Vicars, the soldier who mixed his blood with that of so many other brave Englishmen on the Crimean hills. He was happy, certainly, in his biographer. Without remarkable endowments, without great opportunities, without anything that could be called fame, he shewed Christian devotedness in the trying life of a soldier, and thousands of hearts have been touched and animated by his simple history. Such another was Havelock, the strict Christian soldier, who after many years of obscure duty had at last the glorious end of a hero in the awful crisis of our Indian rebellion. His name, too, is rightly inscribed in the roll of our English saints.

There is another class of recent lives which impress more profoundly, and instruct more largely and usefully, though they do not appeal in the same way to the popular imagination; I mean those of men like Dr Arnold of Rugby and Robertson of Brighton. These lives, that of the former especially, have been of incalculable value to our generation. In them we see men doing intellectual work and grappling with intellectual difficulties in a high spirit of faith and loyalty towards God,—and this in the midst of an intellectual generation. Through a long life of varied work, Arnold is seen uniformly Christian, patriotic, sincere,—always longing to see his country become, and striving to do his best to make it, a true Christian commonwealth. How good a career is that for his country's sons still to contemplate! Robertson's life, shorter but more brilliant and poetical, has the pathos of suffering mixed with it. How noble was his patience, how deeply Christian his aims, how splendid his intolerance of meanness and falsehood and wrong! It is a proud thing for our Church to reckon such a man amongst her loyal ministers. Few lives could do more to elevate the tone of her clergy, and to inspire them at the same time with humility and independence.

To this class of lives has been lately added one of great interest and value,—that of Baron Bunsen, not long since Prussian ambassador in this country. He too, in a profession beset by difficulties, was a sincere and noble-minded Christian. A learned scholar, a laborious diplomatist, he was a man of ardent Christian faith; not merely leading, as some have done, a narrow religious life by the side of his secular employments, but accustomed to look at all the studies of scholars and all the actions of statesmen in the light of Christ, and seeking to offer up his whole being with its entire service on the altar of a purified and enlightened Christianity. Such a life as his, told as it has been by his widow, is an important gift of God to our generation, a seed sown where it may produce most precious fruit.

I have been speaking of lives that have become public property, by being led in conspicuous stations, or at least being described in interesting records. But there have been lives of faith and patience known to us individually, which never drew the eyes of the public upon them, and which have been put into no books. Some persons have been happier in such knowledge than others. There is surely no higher privilege, no greater responsibility, than that of having been brought into close acquaintance with a sincere and resolute Christian life. And it may have fallen to any one's lot to have seen and known persons endowed with the true spirit of the soldier and martyr of Jesus Christ. Even as regards abilities, it has been said, "The world knows nothing of its greatest men;" and this is still truer as regards virtues and graces. The very patience and meekness and contentment which are precious and noble in the sight of God may have helped to keep a life humble and obscure. And there is no human lot, however humble and obscure, in which the qualities of saints may not be tested.

There is always "the world" to be overcome; and this is the victory that overcometh the world, even our faith. To be worldly,—to submit to the opinions and fashions and judgments of the circle in which we live, and to care for the approbation and envy of our world,—is a universal snare, and in some measure, we must say, a universal failing. It is the glory of true saints to overcome the world. A man gains this victory by guiding his own life according to the will of God, according to righteousness and love, and not according to the mere spirit of his day. He gains the victory in a more signal manner if he goes forth to fight against some of the allowed evils in his time, meeting the excuse "It cannot be helped" with the declaration "It is not according to the will of God." Every example of persevering loyalty to the will of God and of confidence in the ultimate dominion of that will is an addition to the blessed company of the saints.

How frequent, again, in every human life, are the calls for exercising *patience*. I have protested that we are not to look for saints only or chiefly in the sick room. But I did not mean that we are wrong in recognizing the virtues tried by sickness and suffering, the virtues of endurance and amiability and resignation, as saintly and admirable. There has been no high Christian virtue, no eminent nobility of life, without patience. Not only those who serve by standing and waiting, but those who speed actively at God's bidding, have need of patience. Disappointment besets with its most cruel blows those who labour most actively in God's service. Sufferings and sorrows are mixed in the lot of all. All have need of patience. And where patience of the true quality has been shewn, a patience sustained by hope, a sweet and kindly patience, there we ought to recognize true saintship. No matter what the circumstances have been, if the patience has been there, there has been the Divine gift and inspiration.

We may all of us feel therefore that the innumerable company of the saints is not a distant body of another nature than ours, but that it reaches even to us in the persons of those, whether they be still with us or have gone before us, who have displayed the like faith and patience. These beckon to us to follow them in hope. We know that they were not perfect; we have seen and criticized their faults: but did they not press onwards? did they not keep a high aim in view? did they not acknowledge the authority of heavenly motives? were they not willing to test all their acts by a heavenly standard? And do we not see, as we contemplate their lives, that they were not victims of a kindly delusion, but servants of a living and righteous Master, who led them, and sustained them, and rewards them? When we commune with ourselves most sincerely, which kind of life seems really the noblest and most to be preferred, that of men who strove and suffered in faith and patience, whether they were happy in this world or not, or that of those who have selfishly steered their course so as always to get the most pleasure and to avoid the most pain?

Brethren, let us try to breathe the better atmosphere of the saints, of the faithful men and women of our race. We have companions around us who would tempt us to live for the present only and to acknowledge the world as our real master. Let us choose a better society. And oh let us beware that in our own influence upon others we are not doing our best to neutralize the example of the saints. Let us not by our habits and aims discredit the testimony of the men of faith and patience. Let us cherish the excellent ambition of being a help and encouragement to others in walking along the heavenly path. Christ himself is the head of the society to which we are invited to attach ourselves. Divine support, Divine inspiration, are at the service of those who are willing to do their best. Let us thank our God for the conditions amidst which he has placed us, for the forerunners whom he has given and points out to us. Let us rejoice that we have brethren whom we may follow, even as they followed Christ.

XII.

COMMON WORSHIP.

MICAH VI. 6.—"Wherewith shall I come before the Lord, and bow myself before the high God?"

THESE phrases, "to come before the Lord," "to bow myself before the high God," denote acts of worship. The words themselves are sufficiently expressive of worship; but it becomes more evident, as the question proceeds, that the inquirer is asking what kind of worship will be acceptable to God. "Shall I come before him with burnt-offerings, with calves of a year old? Will the Lord be pleased with thousands of rams, or with ten thousands of rivers of oil? Shall I give my firstborn for my transgression, the fruit of my body for the sin of my soul?"

But it is to be observed that the worship spoken of is that of the *individual*, not that of the *congregation*.

In all ancient systems of worship means were provided by which worshippers might singly, as individual persons, approach their God. If you recall the institutions of the Jewish temple-worship, you will remember that the rules of sacrifice are, in a very large proportion, made for single persons. The directions in the book of Leviticus begin with the words, "If *any man* of you bring an offering unto the Lord." The Temple was not, in its first intention, a place of meeting. It was the shrine of the one national altar, to which every Israelite, according to the various circumstances of his relation to Jehovah the God of Israel, might bring his offerings. The Levitical law made no provision for regular congregational worship. When the need of regular meetings was felt, *synagogues* or meeting-houses rose throughout the land. But these are not mentioned in the Law, and the uses of them were not confounded in the minds of the Jews with the uses of the Temple. The Temple was for the sacrificial worship of the whole people, regarded as one person, and of the individuals composing the people. Thus Solomon says, in his grand prayer of consecration (2 Chron. vi. 29), "What prayer or what supplication soever shall be made of any man, or of all thy people Israel, when every one shall know his own sore and his own grief, and shall spread forth his hands in this house: then hear thou from heaven thy dwelling-place, and forgive, and render unto every man according unto all his ways, whose heart thou knowest."

You will perceive therefore that the words in our text, "to come before the Lord, and bow myself before the high God," do not correspond exactly to what we say when we speak of "coming to Church." It is worship that is intended in the prophet, but not common or public worship. It is the worship of the individual man, that personal worship which each man owes to the God of all.

This personal worship was rendered, under the Jewish Law, through the form of appointed *sacrifices*. On the significance and the value of this kind of symbolism I do not now propose to dwell. But I may say so much as this, that the language of the prophets shews us that the true significance of the sacrifices was continually being misapprehended, and that therefore instead of being valuable they became mischievous. Such is the danger which besets all forms and expressions of worship—a danger from which no one form or expression in our day more than in any other can boast of being exempt. The Jews, when they forgot the character and mind of their God Jehovah, began to think that they might propitiate him by their sacrifices,—that he cared for the sacrifices in themselves, and, if he received liberal sacrifices, would overlook the wrong-doings of the worshippers. It was the office of the prophets, or inspired preachers, amongst the Jews, to bear witness against this superstition. They proclaimed continually that Jehovah did not care for the sacrifices, but for the mind which accompanied the sacrifices. If the sacrifices were to be substitutes for a right mind and for welldoing, they became not only not acceptable, but abominable. God did not desire them, but hated them. The sacrifices which the Lord God really desired were, a contrite heart, mercy, justice. To this effect is the answer given to the question of our text: "Wherewith shall I come before the Lord, and bow myself before the high God? Shall I come before him with burnt-offerings, with calves of a year old? Will the Lord be pleased with thousands of rams, or with ten thousands of rivers of oil? Shall I give my firstborn for my transgression, the fruit of my body for the sin of my soul?" No: all the rams, all the rivers of oil, if God could be supposed to delight in them, belong to him first, and are his gifts to men. "He hath shewed thee, O man, what is good: and what doth the Lord require of thee, but to do justly, and to love mercy, and to walk humbly with thy God?" These are the offerings in which God delights, justice, mercy, and humility.

As the principles of personal worship, these still abide. If a Christian would render acceptable worship to God, he must strive to do justly and to love mercy and to walk humbly with his God. But in considering the whole passage in the prophet with reference to our condition as Christians, a distinction occurs to us to which I desire to call your special attention. In the Church of Christ, there is no provision, to speak broadly, for that separate personal worship to which a sanction and opportunities were given by the Jewish Law. From the Day of Pentecost, worship in the Church of Christ, so far as it has had any organized expression, has not been single and separate, but *common*. The appointed worship throughout Christendom has always been that of the society, not that of individuals. An Israelite of old came before Jehovah, by the appointment of his national law, with his sin-offering to express his sense of sin, with his thank-offering to express his gratitude: he came by himself, according to the circumstances in which he found himself. The Christian is not invited to come alone; he is taught to approach God always as a member of a body.

The highest act of Christian worship is the joining in the Communion of the Body and Blood of Christ; and this is, as the name Communion testifies, essentially a social or common act. The worshippers gathered together for this, or for the less sacred acts of worship, may be few; but however few they may be, they come together on the ground of fellowship, and represent the principle of society. There is a twofold form of sacrifice proper to our communion-worship,—the offering of thanks and praise, and the offering of gifts or alms. With such sacrifices, as we read in the Epistle to the Hebrews, God is well pleased; and these we are invited to offer as brethren together, as often as we join in the Holy Communion. The rest of our appointed worship,—all that comes under the general head of church-going,—is professedly common, not single. Our book of religion bears as its title the name of the Book of *Common* Prayer.

If there are apparent exceptions to this general statement in the case of the Sacrament of Baptism and the other occasional services, we find on considering the offices for these ceremonies that they are made to the utmost degree social. Whatever is done in church is supposed to be done in the presence and with the assistance of the congregation.

There has been, however, a tendency which we may easily recognize and which we may probably most of us detect in ourselves, to *individualize* our worship, in opposition to the truer spirit of the Church. According to this tendency, the congregation has been an aggregate of persons who joined for convenience to do together what each desired to do for himself. If many persons were to be instructed and exhorted, the preacher might conveniently take them together. The religious exercises which were binding on each, might find a better opportunity through forms of united worship. Whatever most promoted private thought and feeling in the individual would be held to be most edifying in the way of church order. Those who have endeavoured during the last quarter of a century to induce neglecters of church-going to come to church, have often been met by the answer that people could read their Bibles and say their prayers at home; and when they have been dissatisfied with this answer it has been chiefly on account of the suspicion that those who do not come to church are not very fond of pursuing solitary religious exercises at home. But in truth our social worship has a special ground, and a special life, of its own.

It was a marked change, for the first believers in Christ, when the habit of offering sacrifices singly as individuals was abandoned, and only social or common acts of worship were henceforth open to them. But this change accompanied a corresponding new conviction. In being converted they became believers in an invisible Head and Lord. To him they were joined, as they believed, by spiritual bonds, so that they might regard him as continually present with them. Their fellow-believers were joined to Christ by the same bonds. And they were all united together in a spiritual fellowship of a mystical but most close and intimate character. Their life as Christians consisted in realizing this relation to their Lord, and to one another in him. And for those who were most earnest, and in whom therefore we are to look for the character of the early Christian faith, to be a Christian was not merely to take up an opinion which might afterwards be easily dismissed; it was to undergo a mighty change with regard to all the aspects and concerns of existence. All other relations, duties, aims, interests, were as nothing compared with those which centred in Christ. It became therefore a fundamental and permanent conception in the mind of a genuine Christian, to regard himself as bound to his brethren, and as having a share in a corporate life. Remember with what force and frequency St Paul is continually urging this thought upon his fellow-believers. "You are members one of another." This thought is to forbid all sin, to serve as the key and incentive to all duty.

This being one of the most essential characters of the Christian life and calling, and the common partaking of the sacramental bread and wine being handed on to each new Christian society as the most sacred and typical act of worship, it seems natural that it should have been settled, as it were by a deep-rooted instinct, that in the organized system of Christian worship individuals should no longer approach God with solitary devotions, but that whether in confession, or in prayer, or in thanksgiving, or in praise, every Christian should come before God as a member of a family, and thus should learn to know himself as not standing alone in the spiritual world, in the kingdom of God, but as linked in Christ to his fellow-men.

This then is the ground of our social worship. It rests upon that real and actual fellowship with one another which is revealed to us in our common relation to Christ. The more thoroughly any one, from a high moral point of view, looks into the circumstances of human life, the more sure he is to find proofs of this law according to which our Creator has made us. We come into the world sons and daughters, brothers and sisters; we grow to be husbands and wives, parents, friends, neighbours, fellow-countrymen, fellow-worshippers; we are forced to work in union if we would produce any results worth having; we find all the manifestly more delicate and more human faculties of our nature exercised and developed through mutual duties and mutual intercourse. The severest trials, the happiest privileges, of our lives, come to us through our being members one of another. Now this great law is fully declared, and is consecrated to our reverence and submission, in Christ. And we therefore act upon it in Christian worship. We assume that God does not desire to have dealings with us as separate creatures, but will hear us and help us and bless us as partners and brothers. Believing in the communion of saints,—in other words, that God has knit together his elect in one communion and fellowship in the mystical body of his Son Christ our Lord,—we take it as a natural inference that the forms of our worship must represent to the utmost this fellowship.

Common worship, being thus grounded, commends itself by a spirit and life peculiar to it. Every one knows how, under exciting circumstances, a contagion of enthusiasm will spread through assembled multitudes, how one catches fire from another, so that, for great emotions and lofty actions, the bringing of people together is not merely the summing-up of their separate capabilities, but is the development of a new and different power. The striking examples of this effect belong to rare occasions. But in varying degrees it is always natural that emotions cherished in common should be warmer and more animated. Amongst the first Christians it is plain that the meetings for common worship were marked by much warmth and excitement. There is danger attending such excitement. If allowed to spread and advance uncontrolled, it may lead to disorder and other pernicious results. The Christians had experience of this danger, and St Paul is very emphatic in urging that all spiritual emotion must be governed and guided. But he does not object to excitement, even though it be, as it always will be, in part merely physical and nervous. He more than allows it, he encourages it. "Be not drunk," he says, "with wine, wherein is excess; but be filled with the Spirit, speaking to yourselves in psalms and hymns and spiritual songs, singing and making melody in your heart to the Lord." The Apostle is speaking of a pleasure which may be a kind of substitute for the intoxication of wine. Seek, he says, another kind of *fulness*, sensations of enlargement and freedom caused by a higher kind of stimulant. Meet together, and let the Spirit of the one Body possess you. Let music and singing exert their power upon you. Utter the joy and thankfulness which are suitable to your redeemed state in hearty strains of praise.

In ordinary times and unexciting circumstances the fervour of common worship is not likely to be raised to a high pitch. But by observing or remembering what that fervour *may be*, we learn what is the appropriate element or atmosphere of united worship under the most inspiring conditions. And I say it is the privilege of Christians who realize their fellowship in 'one body' to drink into that spirit. The consciousness of a common partaking of the highest gifts and a common seeking of the highest ends should properly generate an atmosphere of joyous and impulsive feeling.

No one is likely to attribute to our congregations in these days any high degree of fervour or enjoyment in worship. We hear frequent complaints, on the contrary, of the dulness and coldness of a decorous Church of England service. Where there is so much repression of feeling, and so little encouragement or opportunity for the display of emotion, it is not easy to say how much individual Christians are inwardly moved by their coming together for worship. I, for my part, brethren, do not doubt that in all congregations where there is reverence and openness of mind, even though they seem listless and uninterested, the Spirit of the body is at work, and something is done by means of the community of prayers and praises to save the souls of the worshippers from losing the sense of brotherhood and sinking into the coldness of selfish isolation. But, on the other hand, is it not obvious that we have been careless about this life and spirit of common worship, and quenched it by indifference, even if we have not turned our backs upon it? Who can say how this spirit might be quickened, if we were resolved to claim our heritage and to open our hearts to the conscious joy of united thanksgiving and praise?

And if our common worship became more inspired, more fervent, and more joyous, it would be more in harmony with this day of rest, with which our worship is so closely associated. It is the Christian custom of *common* worship that has made the Sabbath so expressly a religious day, that we can hardly think of the Sabbath-day as *kept* except by church-going. But if we go back to the Old Testament, in which we find all our exhortations to the keeping of the Sabbath, it is remarkable to find that there the Sabbath-day is hardly associated with *worship* at all, but only with *rest*. And, if our worship were done by each individual singly, there would be hardly any reason for making the day of rest a religious day. But as it is, the day and the custom meet in a beautiful and blessed harmony. The day of common public rest is the opportunity for common worship. As we take our hands off from our ordinary labour, that we may yield ourselves to contemplation and think of him who guides our work and gives us the reward of it, how fit that as Christians we should join our thanksgivings in one, and refresh ourselves together with the remembrance of our common redemption! It is to be regretted that as a general rule we do not find ourselves able between Sunday and Sunday to connect our work still more closely with our worship: but it is fit and natural that the rest-day should be also the great Christian worship-day. Each idea should sustain and throw light on the other. The worship of the day of rest ought to be joyful and refreshing. The rest of the day of worship ought to be thankful and reverent.

We might get rid of the strange contradiction of being afraid of the intrusion of pleasure upon the Sabbath-day, if our recreation and our worship could be more perfectly harmonized, by our worship becoming more of a pleasure, our recreation more thankful and pure.

And now, brethren, if we, remembering our calling as members of Christ, ask the question, Wherewith shall *we* come before the Lord, and bow ourselves before the high God?—we may find the answer plainly written in our New Testament teachers. We may still hear the voice bidding each man in his own life, "Do justly, and love mercy, and walk humbly with thy God!" But when we come as a body of Christian worshippers before God, there are offerings which we are to bring with us, which we are sure will be well-pleasing to God. We must bring with us hearts sensible of our common sins, sensible of our common blessings. We must come repenting together, for ourselves and for each other, giving thanks together for ourselves and for each other. We must come with the true love, the filial and brotherly love, which will knit us to God and to our brethren; with the love which will not be satisfied without expressing itself in uttered praise, in good deeds and oblations. We must come with the hearty resolve to lead more simply the life of sonship, the life of fellowship.

If we could thus come to God with the inward sacrifice, sincerely and naturally expressing itself in the outward tribute, may we not believe that he whom we worship would manifest his acceptance of our offering?

Let me read a passage from the history of the Jewish Temple, which may serve us as a parable: "It came to pass, when the priests were come out of the holy place, and the Levites, the singers, with their sons and their brethren, being arrayed in white linen, having cymbals and psalteries and harps, stood at the east end of the altar, and with them an hundred and twenty priests sounding with trumpets: it came even to pass, as the trumpeters and singers were as one, to make one sound to be heard in praising and thanking the Lord; and when they lifted up their voice with the trumpets and cymbals and instruments of music, and praised the Lord, saying, For he is good; for his mercy endureth for ever: that then the house was filled with a cloud, even the house of the Lord, so that the priests could not stand to minister by reason of the cloud; for the glory of the Lord had filled the house of God."

Yes, my brethren, God will thus meet those who wait upon him humbly according to his will. Let us hope to be rewarded for increased earnestness of devotion with a deeper sense of his presence and of his Fatherly goodness. May he give us the spirit of prayer, in which crying to him as our Father we may find him near to us! May he awaken us out of sleep, and purge our eyes, and quicken us with a stronger life, that we may behold him and cleave to him with true purpose of heart! May our hearts be so wrought upon in this sanctuary, that the natural course of our daily life may be that of doing justly and loving mercy and walking humbly with our God!

XIII.

PREACHING.

St John xi. 9.—"If any man walk in the day, he stumbleth not, because he seeth the light of this world."

LIGHT is given to men in order that they may walk in it and not stumble. The fellowship of our faith demands a corresponding life. It has occurred to me that, as we dwell on this appointed connexion between truth and life, between seeing and doing, the peculiar Christian ordinance or custom of Preaching explains and justifies itself most completely.

The habit of seeing truth and life as naturally connected with one another must have an important effect upon our thoughts concerning truth and life *severally*. When we think of truth, we shall be asking ourselves more or less consciously, How does it bear upon life? What does it tell us as to the way in which we should walk?—When we think of life, we shall be asking ourselves, How far does this or that conduct agree with what we confess to be truth? How shall life be brought into conformity with the truth which we have apprehended? There is this danger in such habitual linking together of truth and life, that a low conception of the one will drag the other down. Speaking generally, unspiritual conceptions of truth will tend to unspiritualize life: and unspiritual conceptions of life will tend to draw the mind towards the less spiritual aspects of truth. But on the other hand if we steadily believe in and keep in view the connexion between truth and life, every higher thought as to the one will exalt the other in our eyes. And the harmony between the two is so real and natural that to be careless of it will lead us almost certainly into insincerity and confusion. All experience proves to us that man lives by knowing, and that he knows in order to live. Knowledge and life,—each continually calls for and solicits the other. Step by step, from the earliest infancy, knowing and doing advance together. The child learns by degrees the laws of nature, and thus at the same time acquires both safety and power. In order to be able to escape from this and to do that, the child is constrained to gain an increasing knowledge of the laws of nature. Spiritual knowledge and spiritual life similarly act and react upon one another from the very beginning. The child learns to recognize a wise and loving will, and so obeys it. By obedience and sympathy the child learns to understand better the will and the reason by which it is guided. Never does any part or province of life become independent of knowledge. There is more appearance of some kinds of knowledge having nothing to do with life. But on consideration we should find that such kinds of knowledge only have *less* to do—not *nothing*—with life; or that they touch life in some way, or at some point, which had not been thought of at first.

As Christians, it is a first principle with us, that the highest Truth and the highest Life are in the closest fellowship with one another. Our knowledge of God is inseparably connected with our inward and our outward life. God is revealed to us in Christ, in order that we may be good Christians. If we desire to be good Christians, we must seek truly to know God; if we become good Christians, we shall be enabled to know God more truly. To see our faith and our life thus mutually requiring each other, is a matter of the greatest importance to us; I do not know whether it is most important for our creed or for our conduct. To consent, however unconsciously, to any division between them, is to condemn ourselves to a dangerous unreality. In that case, our faith will not have the truth and worth to us which it claims to have and ought to have; our conduct will be really prompted by unrecognized motives other than those to which it professes allegiance. A St Paul or a St John saw nothing in the Divine mysteries which did not make an immediate difference to what he himself was to be and was to do. The springs of his daily life were found in his knowledge of God. The reward of his fidelity in life was to be a growth in the knowledge of God.

Now preaching, in the form which it has come

to take amongst Christians, has this office committed to it,—to touch continually the chords by which Divine truth and our common life are connected together.

Preaching, as it exists now, is not, properly speaking, a New Testament ordinance. The word, it is true, occurs in the New Testament; but it misleads us if we attach the same meaning to it there which it has amongst ourselves. It there means "to proclaim:" and it is used to signify the proclaiming of Christ as Lord or Saviour, especially to those who had not heard of him before. Preaching, in this sense, has very little to do with the delivering of sermons twice or three times on Sundays and whenever any number of Christians are assembled for worship. The modern sermon is unknown in the New Testament. It has grown up in answer to the instinctive demands of the Christian community.

Probably not many persons believe, as some seem to do, that sermons are an infliction to which the clergy compel the people to submit. Sermons are really called for by the laity. A hundred years ago, far fewer sermons were preached throughout the country than are preached now. Why has the number of sermons increased? Partly, no doubt, because the clergy, with increased zeal, have desired to preach; but chiefly, because the people, with revived interest in the things of faith, have desired to hear them. It would not be received as a boon by you, brethren, if the sermon at any one of our services were discontinued. We clergymen are sometimes taunted in periodical literature with the length as well as the frequency of our sermons; but we know perfectly well that, on the whole, the great majority of the people do not wish our sermons to be shorter. When that wish becomes general, we shall be sure to conform to it.

Sermons, it is needless to say, must for the most part be all that they are sometimes complained of for being. That is, they must be commonplace; they must be repetitions of what has been said a hundred times before. Why then do people think it good for them to be perpetually hearing sermons? What is the secret of the influence of sermons, such as it is? In what does their virtue consist? Chiefly, I think, and most universally, in this: That they strike the unseen chords which connect together the highest truths and our common life. A very commonplace finger may have just the power to touch those chords. It is a great mistake, in estimating the influence of sermons, to think only of the sermons. The hearers contribute more to the effect than the preacher. This is well understood where there is any great common emotion by which the hearers are possessed, and to which the speaker appeals. But amongst ordinary congregations and in ordinary times, every hearer has a human history of his own. He has his trials, his perplexities, his reasons for joy and sorrow, his causes of fear; he has his sins and his struggles with sin. These particulars are not known to the preacher; but they may make all the difference to the effect of his sermon. I suspect that if each one of us were able to look back over his church-going experience, and to fix upon the sermons which have come home to him most, and in which he has seemed with the greatest awe and conviction to hear God speaking to him, those sermons would not be what others would agree to call the most remarkable or impressive which he has heard, but those which he has happened to hear at critical moments in his own personal history. The preacher may be saying something which passes as mere commonplace through the ears of almost all the congregation; but there may be one heart the soil of which God has himself prepared to receive what is spoken as seed from heaven. The heart may have been softened by sorrow or by thankfulness; the self-conceit may have been taken out of it by humiliation; earthly props and refuges may have abruptly failed; remorse for sin may be imperceptibly gnawing at the inward spirit; a course of thought and inquiry may have led up just to one particular point; doubt of a particular kind may have come to a momentary crisis; and so it may happen that the old familiar testimony to the grace and the righteousness of God the Saviour may come like comfort or warning or guidance specially vouchsafed to the one sinner needing it, and may be bread from heaven to the hungry, living water to the thirsty.

I do not rate lightly the special effects that may be produced by remarkable preaching. It is a grand thing when the Spirit of God rouses masses and generations of men by the voice of an inspired preacher. New aspects of truth, new vehicles of emotion, are necessary to wake men up to hear and to think. It is most desirable that conventionalities of preaching should be broken through and rejected, and that the preacher should strive to speak God's word with all the directness and all the freshness with which the Divine word has a right to be spoken. But in thinking of ordinary sermons and their influence or value, let it be remembered that the hearers of them are not guided or fed or disciplined by the preacher only or chiefly, but by God himself. When has this not been true? In whose case is it not true? The preacher has his opportunity; the spiritual director, where it is attempted to give up the direction of life to a priest, has his greater opportunities: but God's opportunities are more various, his forces are more irresistible, his influence is closer. The truest "direction" for any man is that which leads him to look for God everywhere and to submit to him at all times; it is a most baneful direction which induces a human soul to think of God as only speaking through some one man's voice. Now if you are actually under God's government in your respective lives, and if it is your faith that you ought to know and acknowledge this government, it may be a profitable and a welcome office for sermons simply to bear witness in some way Sunday after Sunday—no need of much novelty for this—to those great unchanging aspects in which God has revealed himself. For we do not see God with our bodily eyes; the truths by which our lives are guided do not force themselves continually upon our senses. We need therefore to be reminded who and what God is, what he has done for us, what he has said to us, what the heavenly vocation is by which we are to live. And even a poor and commonplace preacher, as you and other Christian people feel, may be able to render this service.

The considerations which justify the demand for so many sermons explain also why there should be such sameness of subjects in sermons. There would be a certain attraction, to preachers as well as to some of their hearers, in greater variety. But we remember that we have to speak to a certain number of our fellow-sinners, who might be more or less interested to hear something new, but who are all, as we know,—rich or poor, learned or ignorant, moving much in the world or hardly ever going out of their own houses,—exercised by the greatest and deepest of human experiences. They all know what it is to sin, to be tempted, to be disappointed. They all stumble because they are in darkness, they all want the light of life. When I remember this, I say, Here are the great universal needs, and I ask, Must they not be met with the great universal helps? There is variety in the luxuries of life, hardly in its necessaries. The light of the sun, the air, water, do not weary by their sameness, because they are used for every day's life, worked up into the varying products of human energy and will. And so we preach continually of Christ and the Spirit,—of the Sun of Righteousness who has risen with healing in his wings, of the breath of God which awakens spiritual life and nourishes it,—because Christians of every sort and of every degree are enlightened by the contemplation of Christ and moved by the influence of the Spirit. We can hardly fail to do some good if we only are the means of keeping the image of Christ before so many minds and of naming as Divine that one Spirit of righteousness and peace and joy by which they are conscious of being visited. We cannot convince you unless God convinces you; but we may ask you to look for the light of God, to listen for the voice of God; and as you do this, it may be that you will see that light and hear that voice.

'How dull sermons are, compared with the brilliant compositions which may be read in the newspapers!' Yes, but I am pretty sure that most of you would rather hear sermons when you come to Church, than have those brilliant compositions read to you. And, if what I have already said is true, this is not because you are darkened and enslaved by superstitions, but because you know what you really want. You are all alike in wanting to come near to the great Light of life, to contemplate the ultimate principles of action. You want to go away from Church, if by God's grace you may be so blessed, with more faith, more assurance, a clearer vision of what is right, a more resolute purpose to do it, more hope, more peace, more goodwill towards all about you. Do you really desire this, dear brethren? Then it is not for us to attempt to entertain you with variety. We must, we do, preach Christ to you; Christ crucified, Christ risen; Christ the consecrator of suffering, Christ the hope of glory; Christ the image of the Father, Christ the head of mankind; Christ the judge of our actions, Christ the adviser of our consciences; Christ at the right hand of God, Christ present with us here. Look to Christ, and to God through Christ, and in that light you will see light, you will know where you are, and how you ought to walk.

The guidance which God gives us is well represented by the image of Light, and is not such as can be comprised in any number of precepts. If you look into the Bible for directions what you ought to do in this or that conjuncture, you will probably be disappointed. I do not know in which book of the Bible or in which chapter you would best begin to search. The titles of the sacred books are enough to shew that the Bible is not a volume of directions describing our duties in a complete and systematic form. No good Christian values most those parts of the Bible which consist of precepts. The most precious portion of the Bible by universal agreement is the collection of the four Gospels; and the precepts contained in these are rather casual than formal, profound and universal rather than circumstantial. The chief purpose of the Gospels is to set forth Jesus Christ, and the Kingdom of heaven as he announced it. And this is God's way of teaching us our duty. He shews us in a Life the true principles of human life. He calls us his children; and that we may know what that means, he has revealed himself as our Father through his Son, and at the same time has shewn us in the same person what the filial mind towards God is. All life is a means for us to learn and prove and shew what it is to be children of the true and righteous and loving God, and brethren in Christ towards one another. At any particular time, in any particular circumstances, the question for a Christian to ask is, How shall I serve God's glory best? How shall I come nearest to the Spirit of Christ? It may be extremely difficult to decide; we may need for our judgment the best practical wisdom and knowledge; we may after all, with the best intentions,—or at any rate, with an honest and good intention, as human motives go,—make mistakes. But we shall not permanently go astray if we take the Sun of Righteousness for our light; our mistakes will be turned into valuable lessons for us. By seeing how we have gone wrong in a small matter we may be preserved from erring in a greater matter. And above all things, truth of conscience is the essential need. If we heartily desire to commend ourselves to him who is perfect truth and perfect love, and to be sustained and guided by him, we may trust to him to justify us, both in his own sight and at the right time before our fellow-men also.

XIV.

GIVING BY CALCULATION.

Acts iv. 32.—"Neither said any of them that ought of the things which he possessed was his own."

THERE are two principles, either of which we may act upon in discharging the Christian duty of *giving*.

(1) We may wait till some existing distress, or some good object to be attained, is made to touch our feelings powerfully, and then give under the impulse of the emotion so excited. Or (2) we may make up our minds that we ought to give some proportionate amount of what we have, and then distribute this amount according to our best judgment.

In shorter terms, our giving may be governed either by *feeling* or by *calculation*.

We may think only of the suffering to be relieved and the good to be done; or we may have the conviction, when no appeal is being made to our feelings, that we ought not to spend all that we have upon ourselves.

It is true that we may admit *both* considerations to act upon us, and this I shall presently commend to you as the most excellent way; but it is convenient first to distinguish these from one another.

Now, when any particular benevolent action is to be promoted, the former way, the way of giving when we are moved, may be turned to the best account. We may take our case this morning for an example. We are going to make a collection for our local Dispensary; and I should like the collection to be a good one. If I had no other wish or thought in the matter than that of inducing you to give as much as possible, what should I do? The natural course would be to draw as touching a picture as I could of the sufferings of the poor from sickness. It would not be difficult, without departing at all from truth and observed facts, to exhibit poverty aggravating illness and illness aggravating poverty, till you became softened and unhappy. I could then dwell upon the skill and kindness with which the resources of the medical art are brought to bear upon such suffering by the officers of the Dispensary. I can imagine this being done, —with no departure, I repeat, from truth,—in such a way that it would be a positive relief to your burdened feelings to give, and to give a little more perhaps than you intended when you came into the Church: and so the collection might be made a heavier one. And yet I confess I feel some repugnance to a charity sermon of this sort. So far as I understand what creates the repugnance, it is due to these reasons. (1) Such an appeal, though strictly accurate in its statements, might offend against another sort of truth than that of literal accuracy,—I mean the *truth of proportion*. An exaggerated and unreal conception and state of feeling might be produced, from which there would be afterwards a reaction. (2) There seems also to be a touch of *irreverence* in using such means for such an end. The sufferings of humanity are not things to be trifled with; our own feelings of sympathy are not to be trifled with. I would rather, out of self-respect, that my feelings were not harrowed for the mere end of inducing me to give five shillings or a sovereign. And I would rather, out of respect for others, not dress up the afflictions of our neighbours for the sake of adding ten pounds to a collection. (3) And, if one looks beyond the present occasion, it is to be feared that such exhibitions may harden rather than soften. After being subjected to them once or twice, people know that this kind of thing may be done, and they find it necessary to be on their guard against it. They treat such an appeal as a piece of charitable art. Possibly they get to like a little temporary tragic emotion, and make themselves comfortable by a contribution which they regard as adequate to the occasion.

It is one of the disadvantages of the habit of not giving except when the feelings are strongly moved, that it puts people in a continual attitude of self-defence as regards charitable objects. Prudent persons become possessed by the idea, especially when they think of the multitude of appeals always going about, that there is no safety except in refusing. To give anything they feel would be a sort of letting out of waters. Where is it to stop?—Then this habit, by a kind of natural selection, lets the coldest and most calculating persons escape. They are not weak, and they do not willingly put themselves in the way of appeals, and they have learnt not to believe half they hear; and so it is extraordinary how little is given from one year's end to another by many prudent and well-to-do persons. And, to mention only one other objection to it, this habit places a great temptation in the way of the managers and promoters of charities, making their language sentimental and over-coloured to a degree that may reasonably excite disgust.

The other way of giving is exempt from these disadvantages. But let me speak of some positive advantages attaching to it. The habit of devoting to religious or charitable or public uses a certain proportion of our expenditure is a valuable witness of a twofold claim.

It serves as a practical acknowledgment, in the first place, of *God's* claim upon all that we have. What a man has may have come to him in various ways. He may have earned it for himself or may have received it from others. He may be a rich man, with nothing to do with his money, or a poor man, with many demands upon him. But through all varieties of condition this principle remains constant, that it is by God's permission and gift that every one holds what he has, and no prescription can bar God's primary claim upon it. To the plea, therefore, that a man may do what he likes with his own, it is sufficient to answer that *nothing* is his own to do what he likes with. There is no absolute proprietor but God. All human owners, to use the Scriptural phrase, are stewards.

This truth cannot be stated too strongly or too broadly. Every Christian man, as he contemplates his possessions, is bound to say, These earnings, these profits, these lands, are not mine, but God's. God lends them to me, in order that I may make a good use of them.

But is not this, as some may feel, an unpractical and extravagant claim? Will it not imply that I ought to strip myself of all that I have, and consecrate it to some religious use? It would certainly involve this result, if this were, on the whole, the best application of what you possess. But there are very good and sufficient reasons for believing that it would *not* be the best use that any of us could make of what he has, to give it all away to the poor or to the Church. In that case we should not, by so doing, be rendering up to God that over which he has a claim. But we are none of us exempt from the obligation of considering how we may best apply to the carrying out of God's will the means with which he has intrusted us.

Now the question what use we should make of our money is by no means an easy one to settle. When it is asked in the court of conscience, How shall a man spend? how much, and to what, shall he give?—let him who finds it easy to answer call it easy. To me it seems that the matter is full of difficulties, and that there are objections to almost every general rule that can be laid down. But there are two great considerations which come home to the mind with peculiar force. It suits the wellbeing and progress of society on the whole that people should spend most of their income, with such taste and judgment as may be given them, on the necessaries and comforts and luxuries of life. This may be called a law of nature, which no other law manifestly steps in to override. When we see therefore richer people spending more than poorer on houses and the like, there is no reason why we should say, This is not in accordance with God's will. The other consideration is that it has always been a rule, denied by no one, felt most strongly by the best men, that a man should spend a part of what he has in trying to do good, that is, upon objects and aims outside of the circle of his own personal and family interests. These two conclusions we may regard as placed beyond doubt : (1) that in ordinary cases we are justified in spending the greater part of our income, so to say, upon ourselves ; and (2) that it is not justifiable for any one to spend the whole of his income upon himself.

Now if any one lays down a rule for himself to *give* such or such a proportion of his income, he is acknowledging in the most practical manner that, as an owner of money, he is under obligations,— that his means are not his to do just what he likes with, but that he is bound to consider how to use them wisely and well. The simple resolution to give so much as a matter of duty will react upon the man's whole conception of property, helping him continually against the mischievous and unchristian notion that because other men may not take his money from him at their pleasure *therefore* he has an absolute right over it. Just as the rule of giving certain hours to formal *worship* is a useful witness to us that all our hours should be really given to the service of our Maker, so the rule of devoting a certain sum to good and charitable purposes may remind us that all our expenditure should be so regulated as to promote the glory of God.

And there is this advantage in contributing our charitable gifts in the serious manner provided for us by our Communion offertory as express offerings to God, that it condemns all feelings of levity and vanity and patronage in giving, and reminds us that to give is a solemn duty, and that in giving we are only rendering up by a deliberate and voluntary act of sacrifice a part of what God has first bestowed upon us.

The other claim to which I referred as being recognized by a rule of giving away a certain proportion of our income, is that which our brethren have upon us. There is only a distinction in aspect, not in reality, between this claim and that of which I have been just speaking. But it is important that we should recognize the obligation under this aspect. We very much exaggerate our supposed rights to the free enjoyment of what we own. We really receive what we have from the community, and we owe it to the community again. The only thorough justification of private property from the moral point of view is in its being made to serve the public good. Now, when a man says, 'I set apart so much of my income in order to do good if I can to the less favoured members of my community or of my race,' he is helping himself to remember that he holds all his property upon the tenure of making it serviceable to his country and to mankind. This conviction will not require you to surrender all that you possess to some public or charitable uses, because the good of society would not be so furthered. But it may influence strongly and decidedly what you do with your money, and the more it is allowed to have its due influence on your conduct, the better: for it is certainly true in the eyes of God that every man's right of private ownership, be he the wealthiest duke or a labouring man, is controlled and subordinated, as it is also in reality sustained, by the higher right which society has to the utmost benefit which every member of it has the means and opportunities to render.

We ought then to say to ourselves habitually, 'These poverty-stricken people, these uneducated, these neglecters of ordinances, have claims upon me. I cannot thrust them aside with the sneer, Am I my brother's keeper? I and my money exist in part for them. Can I suppose that He who made both them and me had no purpose in giving me more money and other advantages except that I should enjoy myself with them? I will at any rate be mindful that I do not withhold from my poorer brothers such benefits as a reasonable liberality on my part may help to confer upon them.'

Let us not overrate what money can do. The giving of money is very far from being a discharge of our obligations to our fellow-men. We owe them more and better things than money. And it is a mistake to suppose that by giving money enough we can do as much good as we please. The best services to the world have not been rendered by money or by what money could buy. We soon discover the weakness of money in the work of doing good. But it must be admitted that there are few things which test and exercise the inner nature of a man so much as his use of his money. There are many mysteries of human nature connected with ownership and spending. So large a part of human activity is employed not only in the getting, but in the holding and spending of money, that man might be described as a spending animal. A great deal of character, a great deal of virtue or of weakness, is shewn in every man's relations to what he owns. It is no trivial matter therefore as a moral act, not a duty which any one can look down upon as insignificant, to resolve carefully and cheerfully to apply a substantial proportion of income to religious and charitable uses. Such action, you may depend upon it, will tell upon the whole spiritual nature.

Need I say, that the increased prevalence of such a custom would soon shew itself in the swelling of the streams of our charitable resources? Most persons give much less than they fancy they do. Partly from that attitude of self-protection to which I have alluded, and partly from the time and trouble which it costs them to make up their minds to give a moderate sum, many not unkindly persons are under the impression, which their account-books would correct, that they have given, say within the last year, a good deal more than they have. A rigorous inquiry, Have I given such or such a proportion of my spendings? would be likely to lead to a paying-up of considerable arrears.

I have not named any particular proportion of income which it may be right to set apart for giving. There is one proportion which Scripture and tradition combine to suggest; but I know of no principle which makes that proportion of one-tenth binding, and I confess it to be extremely difficult to find conclusive reasons for one proportion more than another. There is some guidance perhaps in this fact, that if a considerable majority were to give anything like one-tenth, the administrators of voluntary offerings would have more than they would know what to do with. We sometimes boast of the largeness of these offerings, but at such times we generally forget how immense our wealth is. There may well be variety in the proportion given, as there is variety in circumstances and in warmth of liberality. I have known of persons giving away a third part and even more of their income. But I should expect it to be a great advance in liberality with most, if they began to give a twentieth part. And I should not at all object to their ascertaining what part of their *rates* goes to the actual relief of the poor, and then reckoning that as a part of their charity. The most real difficulty, let me say, is in the case of those who have hardly been able to make a bare provision for their children, and who feel it a duty to lay by almost everything that they seem able to spare for the future support of those who depend upon them.

One argument more in favour of this habit of giving deliberately a proportion of income. It would lead to thought and discrimination in giving. It is better for society, though apparently not for themselves, that people should spend their money in any ordinary way than that they should give it foolishly. An incredible amount of moral harm is easily done by carelessness in giving. It is difficult to believe this. It seems perplexing that so good an emotion as that of compassion should lead to so much moral evil. But the fact that it may do so is only too certain to those who have had any experience in such matters. And when once this has been learnt, it is positively culpable to give way to simple feeling, and to relieve apparent distress without knowing what the effect of the relief is likely to be. It is a most desirable thing that Christian and humane persons should be led to consider how they may best apply what they have made up their minds to give. To judge rightly in this question is a high and excellent wisdom; but to try to judge rightly is a wholesome exercise, and likely to promote reverence, humanity, and a sense of responsibility. The extension of such a practice, together with the increase of the amount to be given, would probably lead to the choice of good *public* objects for the exercise of liberality, rather than to any considerable addition to the amount spent on feeding the poor.

I have been arguing, as you perceive, against the uncontrolled sway of feeling, and in favour of calculation, in this matter of giving. Is, then, Christian liberality, Christian charity, of all things in the world, to be turned into mere arithmetic? Is emotion to be suppressed, in order that our beneficence may be done mechanically? That would indeed be a strange doctrine to preach in a Christian Church. I will not draw back from what I have said in favour of calculation. But I venture to believe that feeling may be kept alive more healthily with the guidance and the support of calculation. I would have you, my brethren, still susceptible to every cry of distress. I would have you never turn away your face in hardness and indifference from any poor man. Let the feeling excited in you by any suffering which you may see or hear of set you considering whether you can do anything to relieve it. If in some way, it may seem by mere chance, this or that kind of suffering, this or that good to be aimed at, be brought specially home to you, take that as an indication of Divine Providence, and believe it to be legitimate and right for you to exert yourself and to give in that particular way. Some teachers, holding as I do that it is well to set apart a certain proportion to good works, have said that those who are deeply moved may fitly indulge their feelings by giving something in excess of that which in their coldest and most prudent moments they have set apart. And always, if we do not give more in money, it is a good thing to be stirred beyond the giving of money. By prayers, by sympathy, by some uncalculated moral action, we may often give far more precious aid than if we were to multiply our money contributions tenfold.

The great thing would be, my Christian brethren, that we should arrive by God's grace at such a state of mind as that indicated in the words of my text, "Neither said any of them that ought of the things that he possessed was his own." A man, and the things he possesses, are very closely bound up together. It is very hard to weaken the mysterious ties of this binding. Let us try another way. Let the man give *himself first*, and then he will give, with himself, whatever he has. Let him give himself to God, to his fellow-men. St Paul was not content with saying, What you have is not yours; he went further and said, " *Ye* are not your own." If we have learnt that lesson, we have learnt all. If we are inwardly persuaded that we have been bought with a price, so that we belong body and spirit to God, we shall have no mind to withhold anything that God asks of us from him.

Let me add a few words to connect what I have said with another subject. We are entering to-day upon an election week. I have nothing to say to you about the election itself. But the stir of an election brings home thoughts of politics to the minds of all. Now in all politics, whatever side we take, and whether we have much or little to do with politics, there is one consideration which I may urge as never out of place. We ought always to cherish the desire to help the weak and to serve the common good. The politician, the statesman, most deservedly honoured in the long run, whether he has been called Whig or Tory, Conservative or Liberal, has been he who has sympathized with the unprosperous, and has earnestly desired to exalt the brothers of low degree. To take the side of those who are pushed out of the way is the cultivated sentiment of the true gentleman, the proper instinct of the common man: it is, above all, the duty and grace of the Christian. If we do not cherish the sense of responsibility towards and on behalf of the humblest, we are no followers of him who emptied himself of Divine glory and took upon him the form of a servant,—who, though he was rich, yet for our sakes became poor. May the Christian spirit be poured out upon all parties and all classes, that our country may prosper and be at one!

XV.

PUBLIC AND PRIVATE EXPENDITURE*.

1 Cor. iv. 7.—"What hast thou that thou didst not receive?"

In a country not yet civilized, or in one decaying back into anarchy, where the stronger and bolder could seize with impunity the possessions of the weak, and where the poor were therefore liable at any time to be plundered either in the name of government authority or in defiance of it, it might be the duty of the preacher to do what he could to foster the idea of the sacredness of private property, so as to strengthen the barriers of custom and opinion against injustice. But the preacher's duty alters with circumstances. In our country at the present time there is no need to preach on behalf of the rights of property. Law is omnipotent here against violence. The traditions of many generations of settled possession have given prodigious strength to the claims of property, and there is hardly anything so practically and universally sacred in an Englishman's eyes as the right of a man to hold fast his own and to do what he likes with it against every kind of interference. Respect for the

* One of a course of political sermons preached at St Mark's, Whitechapel.

rights of private property has grown into an undue reverence for those rights. There is a widely prevailing notion that to secure each man in the enjoyment of what he can call his own is an ultimate end for which society and its institutions exist. The rights of private property, therefore, need no support from the English preacher. His advocacy is wanted at the present time for another doctrine,—that the individual and his property exist rather for the common or public good.

I speak in this place as a minister of the Gospel of Christ, whose first and proper business it is to consider how the teaching of that Gospel bears upon any subject which he may have in hand. The political philosopher would inquire what grounds there are in nature and history and utility for the unquestioning reverence so commonly paid to the right of private ownership. It is enough for me to ask what are the ideas which the New Testament encourages, and what therefore should be the ruling prepossessions of the Christian mind, on this subject of property.

There is one great support given by the New Testament to the security of personal ownership. It repeats the old commandment, "Thou shalt not steal," and reinforces it with the argument drawn from that spiritual fellowship of men which is revealed in Christ. More generally, the New Testament is in favour of justice, order, and government. It absolutely condemns fraud and oppression and everything that could rightly be called robbery of private persons. Wherever the principles of the Gospel might prevail, they would secure that every one should dwell safely under his own vine and his own fig-tree. But beyond this, you will not find in Holy Scripture any honour paid to the principle of private property. It is never spoken of there as the basis of the social system. You could never learn from the Bible the habit of reverencing private property, of making it the primary consideration in social arrangements, of consenting that important ends should be sacrificed out of deference to it.

On the contrary, possessions (including, as one may say, the very principle of possession,) are treated with systematic and surprising depreciation by our Lord and his Apostles. You may perceive throughout their words an endeavour to resist and overcome the natural feeling of respect for possessions. Property is spoken of as a false god, which men are dangerously tempted to worship. A man's life, we are taught, consists not in the abundance of the things he possesses. The disciples of Jesus are bidden to seek treasure in heaven and not in earth. The rich are seldom mentioned without disparagement. Riches are a snare, the love of money a root from which all evil may grow. We are told in a parable of a rich man who said to his soul, "Soul, thou hast much goods laid up for many years: take thine ease, eat, drink, and be merry. But God said to him, Thou fool, this night thy soul shall be required of thee: then whose shall those things be which thou hast provided?"

There is a simple theory consistently assumed in the New Testament concerning possessions of every kind. However acquired, whether by inheritance or gift or labour, they are entrusted by God to the possessor. Man is a steward, bound to make such use of what he possesses as may satisfy the real owner. Faithfulness in this stewardship is strictly demanded. And the use of property which God prescribes is to lay it out for the common benefit. If we are not to sell all that we have and give the price to the poor, we ought to be able to shew that we can do better not only for ourselves, but for the poor also, by making some other use of the money. We use money rightly when we "make friends" by means of it,—that is, when we confer benefits and promote unity and good feeling. A man will take the true view of his possessions if he says, These things belong, not to me, but to God and to my brethren. The broadest statement of this doctrine is that which lays down that each man himself belongs to God and to his brethren; then money is one of the instruments with which he works, one of the talents which he is charged to invest. And in order to shew the Christian theory of property at work in an example, the ordinary laws of human life were suspended for a moment at the first creation of the Church, and the newly inspired believers were constrained to make an actual surrender of all claims of ownership. "The multitude of them that believed were of one heart and of one soul; neither said any of them that ought of the things which he possessed was his own; but they had all things common."

Now what are our reflections when we are reminded of this teaching?...'A system of communism is not suited to the present condition of society; it was but a momentary phenomenon in those first Pentecostal days.'...Granted. But are we then to dismiss the whole teaching of Scripture on this subject as unpractical, and to ground ourselves in some different philosophy? There is no sufficient reason for our thus setting at nought, on a point of intense and universal interest, the authority which we deem most sacred. It may be maintained on the contrary, that if our common notions were brought more into harmony with the New Testament, they would be worthier of a free and civilized people, and would conduce to the unity and stability of our country.

The effect of the Scriptural teaching, if it were allowed to operate upon our convictions, would be to alter in some degree the relative standing, to our minds, of the public good and of private interests. It would tend to elevate the former and to depress the latter, and so to increase the proportion contributed by individual possessors to the public and to diminish that expended upon themselves.

It may be a surprise to some persons to hear the amount of what we contribute in this country towards public objects treated as inadequate. Our contributions are of two kinds, compulsory and voluntary,—what we pay in rates and taxes, and what we give in subscriptions or otherwise. We are apt to think that we are heavily taxed, and that we give very largely. But neither supposition is right, if we compare England with other countries, and if we take into account the great wealth of this country. A traveller coming to our shores from any other country in the world, and observing our public and private expenditure, would be certain to be struck by the splendour of our private displays as far surpassing the beauty and perfectness of our public arrangements. This metropolis of ours is a marvellous city, but rather on account of the unparalleled number of rich and well-to-do people who are gathered here and spend their money in various ways according to their tastes, than because we can be proud of it as a richly adorned capital. There is much that is extremely and needlessly mean in London. No one living here would think of saying that Londoners or other Englishmen give their minds much to making London one of the noblest capitals in the world. But this is what it ought to be. We have money enough to make it so. This capital and our other great towns ought to be enriched with every beauty and comfort which can be procured for money. Our rural districts, again, would make the same impression upon our traveller. Our parks and mansions are unequalled in the world. But almost everything that strikes the observer as specially delightful is private property. The condition of the rich is all that they could desire. But in many parts the condition of the labouring class is comfortless and depressed to a degree which the luxuries of private houses make only more painful. To say the least, there is very little deliberate outlay in our country districts with a view to making the life of the common people a happier one. But something, surely, might be attempted in this direction, if we cared enough about it.

I am speaking of what may be called our domestic public expenditure, such as is chiefly provided for by our rates, but partly also out of our national funds, and partly from voluntary contributions. One of the most interesting and important items in this home public expenditure is the sum invested in education. We do not at present * pay for education out of local rates; the cost of it, so far as it is of a public character, is provided partly by an annual grant from the national funds, partly from endowments, and partly from voluntary subscriptions. In these days nations in which there is much concern for the public interests spend freely on education; but in this way of spending we—to our shame it must be said—are most niggardly. I do not know why we should be behind any nation in the world in efforts to raise the whole mass of our citizens: but I am afraid to say how much we are behind—say Switzerland or the United States. This is not the place for details. But I will take by way of illustration, and for the sake of

* This was written before the passing of the Elementary Education Act.

comparison, one fact, which we shall most of us find it very difficult to believe. In all parts of the United States the people are used to being heavily rated for public objects; and perhaps there is no place in that country in which there is greater concern for the general wellbeing and for the elevation of the lower classes than there is in Boston. Now in Boston, as we learn from the Report of our recent Schools Inquiry Commission, the local tax, answering for the most part to our rates, is estimated as amounting to a rate of 20 per cent. on income, of which the School tax is generally about one-third. What should we think of that? What would a family spending £300 a year think of having to pay a rate of £20 a year towards public schools? The result of this tax is that schools good enough for the children of the rich are thrown open free to the poorest. The poor have the boon for nothing. The richer who pay the tax, when they have large families, get their money's worth in the schooling. The burden falls on those who can best afford to bear it.

We are apt, as I said, to think our rates already heavy. In some parishes in the East of London they are said to be overwhelming. Morally speaking, rates are no doubt always heavy. But as a matter of arithmetic, a rate of so much in the pound means that, whilst we are spending the main part of our income in private ways, we are called upon to spend so much for the advantages of paving and lighting and police and the like, and so much for the maintenance of the poor. Now if we calculate what we get for our money, and try to realize what we receive in return for the £5, or the £10, or £20, which we pay in rates, it is impossible that any other things we get for the same sum should appear to us so good a money's worth. Such is the advantage of combination. The same consideration does not apply to what is raised for the maintenance of the poor. But this is not really so heavy as it looks. If the ratepayer will ascertain what proportion of what is called his poor-rate is strictly for the poor, and then will compare this with his income, he may be as unwilling as ever to pay a shilling more than is necessary or advisable; but he will hardly find the sum itself an overwhelming one. I should be surprised to learn that there are many ratepayers who in the worst times have paid as much as £2 per cent. of their income towards the support of the poor,—as much, that is, as $\frac{1}{10}$th part of what the people of Boston pay for their local expenditure.

I am no advocate, however, for spending more upon the direct relief of the poor. If it were good, indeed, for the indigent themselves that they should have more relief, the principles I have been urging upon you would compel us to give it ungrudgingly. But no one can see much of the working of public charity or of any kind of almsgiving, without becoming most painfully impressed with the risk that there is of demoralising whole classes of society by simply making it easier for them to obtain relief when they are in want. The countries where there is the most liberal public spirit do not spend much upon feeding the poor. It is at least as important to be judicious as to be liberal in giving. And there is positive evil in allowing people to make themselves dependent upon either public or private charity more than can possibly be helped. I should be proud to see larger rates willingly paid, but not for the relief of the poor. They should go towards education and public improvements of every kind.

Still, it will be objected, many of the ratepayers are very poor, and they would be crushed by any increase of the rates. That would be a lamentable consequence, and is certainly one to be avoided. I should only wish, when the pressure of rates is spoken of, that it should be reduced to arithmetic, and that it should be clearly seen what proportion of income (not merely how much in the pound of rent) is demanded for the numerous and most important public advantages which the rates provide. No rate was ever dreamt of in this country but was slight in its pressure compared with the cost of other necessaries required by a family. Those who are crushed by the rates are also crushed at the same time more effectually by their butchers' or bakers' or grocers' bills. But if we cannot find it in our hearts to lay more upon the poorer ratepayers, there is the alternative of *laying it on the richer*. Our economists are very much afraid of propositions for taxing the rich more heavily. They condemn most strongly the policy adopted in ancient Athens, of making people pay an increasing rate on a larger property, so that the richer man should not only pay more, but a larger proportion, than the poorer. And we owe great deference to their objections. But in all free states there will be and must be arrangements, such as we are already in some degree familiar with, to relieve the poorer citizens in some measure from the weight of public burdens. And it seems intolerable that the expenditure of a great country on important public objects should be regulated by the poverty of the poor class rather than by the wealth of the rich.

In the free states of antiquity the wealthy citizens were made to feel, by the traditions which surrounded them from their birth and by the common opinion of their countrymen, that their country had claims on them and their wealth which they must seriously set themselves to discharge. Although so much was exacted from them in the way of taxation,—or partly, perhaps, *because* they were taught by these demands,—they were accustomed to vie with one another in magnificent voluntary outlays for the benefit or the delight of the public. Every man's "talent" was expected to be at the service of his country, and the rich man's talent was his wealth. Can it be said that such a conviction prevails at all generally amongst our rich men? If it does not, is not this a sign of the comparative weakness of the public interest when matched against the tenacity of private ownership? Very moderate subscriptions will win a man a good character for charitable liberality. Class feeling has considerable power in extracting large sums of money, as when a man holds himself bound to fight an election contest at an immense cost for the sake of his party. But where do we discern, amongst our crowds of rich people who are always spending against each other and daily inventing new forms of extravagance, a generous rivalry in endowing their country with gifts of use or beauty? The spectacle of a great fortune destroyed by folly and profligacy is, I am afraid, more common than the devotion of equal revenues to the public service. Three examples of such munificence readily occur to our minds,—three when there might be fifty,—the noble gifts of Miss Burdett-Coutts, Mr Peabody, and Mr Whitworth; and of these three one is an American. Let us not withhold from them the honour which is the more due to these individual benefactors because they are so few. But it would be well at the same time if we could diffuse the impression that these few millionnaires are only doing what hundreds more ought to do. We ought not to worship money with too profound a reverence even in its best form of liberal gifts. It would be useful, I believe, to put into circulation a demand that the wealth which the country has in fact given to the rich should be in part returned by them to the country in well-chosen schemes of munificence, and a grave social condemnation of those who glory in their riches as though they had not received them. And this is my justification for speaking to a Whitechapel congregation of the duty of great proprietors.

I am unwilling to believe that there is any decay of essential public spirit in the minds of Englishmen. It would be grievous to be driven to the conclusion that we of the present age, who have inherited a greater accumulation of treasures, care less than our fathers did for this England of noble memories, and are more inclined to grudge to our country the devotion of our individual selves. If our public spirit seems inactive, let us say hopefully, It is not dead but sleepeth. If a great crisis were to come, to die for his country would still be held to be the plain duty of every citizen. But we are called upon now, I venture to urge, not to die for our country, but to do the harder thing—to live for it. And as to live is in great part to spend, I commend to you the duty and discipline of spending on the public interests. There is a great strain and pressure of political teaching in the opposite direction. To keep down the rates, which may mean one of two things,—either to prevent extravagance and waste, a most laudable object, or to cause that the inhabitants shall spend less on public improvements and the poor, that they may have more to spend upon themselves and their families,—is regarded without discrimination as an unqualified virtue. It is proclaimed that Parliament ought to cut down the public revenue, and then tell the

Government that they must do as well as they can with what remains. Encouragement is given to the notion that education must be left to be starved in the poorer districts by the method of voluntary subscriptions. There seems to me to be a different ideal of public policy,—not to repel every higher interest and pride of the members of the commonwealth from public action, not to regard the country as having its being mainly in order that individuals may grow rich and enjoy themselves, not to labour that the expenditure supplied by taxes and rates shall be limited to the barest necessities of national existence, and shall cover nothing splendid, nothing fruitful of popular happiness and wellbeing,—but to aim sedulously at making our country one of which we and our children may be prouder, to give heart and mind to the devising of public improvements and to grudge no money that may be needed to carry them out, to call upon and to train our population to bear as cheerfully as other free nations have done the burdens of a noble State.

XVI.

THE IRISH CHURCH QUESTION[*].

MICAH VI. 8.—"He hath shewed thee, O man, what is good; and what doth the Lord require of thee, but to do justly, and to love mercy, and to walk humbly with thy God?"

THE subject on which I am about to speak to you this morning, my brethren, is that which is well known to have become the leading political question of the day, and which promises to occupy the public mind in an engrossing manner for some time to come. You will understand that I refer to the Irish Church question.

I make no apology for referring to politics in the pulpit. I believe, indeed, that it is not often expedient to give up a sermon entirely to a political topic. A preacher who considers the wants of the whole congregation finds himself constrained for the most part to keep to Bible texts, and to the great sacred subjects which concern all men and women, and which have power to interest them most profoundly. But it is on every ground right and good—it is good for us as Christians, good for us as citizens—to connect together our politics and

[*] This Sermon was preached before the General Election by which the question of the Irish Church Establishment was decided.

our devotions; and there are occasions on which the politics of the time claim more than a passing allusion in the exhortations of the preacher. When the whole country is called upon to choose a particular policy, and a public opinion of all classes is to be formed, we may expect that the political question will commend itself to the congregation generally as both important enough and interesting enough to be made the subject of a sermon. And this is now the case with regard to the legislation to be adopted in the matter of the Irish branch of our Church.

My purpose is not, I can confidently say, to urge my own opinions upon your acceptance. Nor is it primarily to give such suggestions as may lead to the formation of a right opinion. I write and speak, as you will believe, in the seriousness impressed on me by a twofold responsibility. I remember first the obligations which rest upon one who speaks in so sacred a place and so sacred an atmosphere. And I remember also that I speak to persons who have formed, it may be with strong conviction, different opinions; and who, as they are constrained to listen with respectful silence to what is preached here, may certainly claim that the pulpit of our English Church should not be used for the purposes of partisanship. What may be done with advantage here, and what I aim at, is this, to bring our views and our reasons into the highest light. Every one knows that, on all sides, many less worthy impulses mix with the prosecution of political objects. There is a spirit of party, there are rough and stubborn prejudices,—not to speak of baser alloys,—from which it is idle to expect any political movement to be exempt. Here in the Church, as in our closets, the question to ask ourselves is not, What do we like? nor, What does party allegiance demand? but, What is right in the sight of God? What is the policy most becoming to students of the Scriptures and to disciples of our Lord Jesus Christ? Here I may beg you, whatever your opinions may be, to consider what objects persons of all opinions ought to regard as paramount, and what principles all must be careful not to violate.

That the country should come to the right conclusion upon any controverted question is the point of most obvious practical importance; but it is a matter of scarcely secondary consideration that the contest should be carried on with a constant reference to high principles. And this is especially to be thought of when the question, like that now before us, is one which involves the interests of religion and of the Church. To neglect and surrender high interests, out of carelessness or worldliness, is a bad thing; but to support a sacred cause in a spirit of blind and factious partisanship is perhaps a worse thing.

Within the last few months, then, we have been brought face to face with a problem which has loomed distantly for some time. What the exigencies of political warfare may have had to do with forcing on the issue, is a matter which does not concern us here. The question is grave enough to demand to be settled on its own merits. What we perceive is, that it has been resolved by one of the great parties in the State, with the support of a majority of the House of Commons, to put an end to the political ascendancy of the Church now established in Ireland, in the name of justice to the Roman Catholic population, and in order to remove one of the causes of the disaffection which unhappily prevails in that country. On the other side, an appeal is made to the constituencies to maintain the existing status of that Church.

The Protestant Church in Ireland is a part of our own Church. When we look at the title-page of our Prayer-book, we find that our worship is arranged "according to the use of *the United Church of England and Ireland.*" So far as doctrine and discipline and government are concerned, the Church in Ireland stands on exactly the same footing as the Church in England. If we were to go into any part of Ireland, we should find ourselves in a parish like an English parish, with a clergyman ordained like an English clergyman, under a Bishop appointed by the Sovereign as in England, and with all our Anglican services performed in the Church. An attack on the Church in Ireland is therefore an attack on a member of our own body. We may justly be called upon to sympathise with our fellow-believers and fellow-Churchmen in Ireland when they are in any adversity. We may be justly asked to consider whether it is honourable, and whether it is for our own safety, to surrender an outpost because it is weak and surrounded by enemies.

There are many personal ties by which the Church in Ireland is linked to the Church in England. People move from Ireland to England, from England to Ireland, and have been accustomed to find themselves surrounded by the same Church system. Families live partly on this side of St George's Channel, partly on the other. An English clergyman of distinction becomes an Irish prelate; an Irish clergyman becomes an eminent English preacher. Are all these living ties, it is asked, to be ruptured?

Another strong bond of sympathy unites the great majority of English Church-people to their Irish brethren. We most of us live in great fear and horror of Romanism; and Irish Protestantism is an encampment in the midst of Romanism. Ireland is substantially a Roman Catholic country, and its religion is of an excessively Roman or Ultramontane character. Naturally, this religion is not very favourable to loyalty; and it is notorious that there is a strong tendency to disaffection running through the Irish Roman Catholic population. Can we have the heart to take away a single privilege from our loyal fellow-Protestants thus beleaguered by Popery and disaffection?

Such appeals cannot fail to have influence, and surely ought not to be without influence, on right-thinking and right-feeling persons.

On the other hand, we are reminded that we are not only members of the English Church, but also citizens of the British Empire. And it is in the latter character that we are now called upon to deliberate and to act. The question is not with what feelings English Churchmen ought to regard their Irish brethren, but what policy the Government of Great Britain ought to pursue towards Ireland. In a free country like this, we, the population generally, through public opinion and our representative institutions, determine the action of the Government. We cannot therefore put off our responsibility, and say we will have nothing to do with public policy. God and our country have charged us with a greater or less burden of responsibility. Still less is it open to us to express an opinion, and to vote, and so practically to take a part in the government of the Empire, and yet to plead that we act only as sympathising fellow-Churchmen and fellow-Protestants, and take no account of the public interests and of the claims of fellow-subjects whose creed is not the same as ours.

As citizens of the British Empire, then, (it is said,) we are responsible in our degree for the just and good government of every part of the Empire. Past history has made the British Crown supreme over populations of various races and beliefs. We govern in India, for example, vast multitudes of Mussulmans and Hindoos. We have Roman Catholic fellow-subjects, and Presbyterian fellow-subjects. The governing class in this great Empire still belongs predominantly to the English Church; but no one who is not totally ignorant of history and politics supposes that it is possible in the government of the Empire simply to carry out our own religious prepossessions, and to take no account of the faiths of our fellow-subjects. We are *compelled* to remember—even if every just and sensible man did not willingly remember—that the natives of India are Hindoos and Mussulmans, that the Scotch are Presbyterians, that the Maltese are Roman Catholics. It is no easy matter—this every one will allow—to govern wisely and well such a complex Empire as ours. It is impossible to enforce one system of organization through the whole. But we or our ancestors have chosen to have such an Empire; so far as we ourselves at this moment are concerned, Divine Providence assigns it to us, with the responsibility of doing our best for it. The more troublesome and perplexing the government of it is, the more evidently is it necessary not to impose the same constitution, civil or ecclesiastical, upon every part of it, but to consider anxiously and with docility what justice and good policy in each particular case may prescribe. There may easily be differences of opinion as to what is just or politic; there can be but one opinion that we ought to try to find out and to do what is just and politic with reference to the circumstances of each part of the Empire.

In any new case, we are able to see tolerably alike. I have alluded to Malta. That is a small island, of which England has become possessed, containing a bigoted, and not, I believe, particularly well-affected, Roman Catholic population. We occupy Malta with a strong garrison, civil as well as military. We carry our own religion with us. We have there churches and clergymen, and occasionally a Bishop. But no one proposes that the whole island should be cut up into parishes, and that an Anglican ecclesiastical establishment sufficient to supply the native population, if they would use it, should be planted there. Every one feels that the religion of the natives must be respected, and that it would be both unjust and impolitic for the British Government to ignore it.

Now in Ireland—so it is urged by those who are promoting a change of policy in that country—the native population is in the main Roman Catholic. If English and Scotch settlers, and their descendants, were excepted, there would be few Protestants in Ireland. The adherents of the Church of England form a small minority—fewer, I think, than one in seven—of the population. But the Anglican Establishment is arranged on a scale which assumes that the whole country comes under its care. There are twelve Bishops for a population less than that of one of our larger English dioceses. There are parishes in which there are hardly any Protestants except the clergyman and his family. The State provides religious instruction and the means of worship for the Irish people; but they are of a kind which the Irish people—that is to say, both the immense numerical majority and those who are most properly Irish—reject with deep-rooted aversion. It happens also that those who accept the State provision are the wealthier portion of the community, those who reject it the poorer. The rich and partly alien minority are endowed by State bounty, the poor native population have to support their own religion out of their private resources.

These are undisputed statements, and the state of things which they describe is so admittedly unsatisfactory that the most enthusiastic defenders of the Irish Establishment generally allow that if we were beginning with Ireland now it would not be reasonable to institute the existing Church system there. It is a different thing, they say, to cause a great social disturbance for the sake of remedying a disproportion. This plea is sure to have considerable weight in this country. We are so used to disproportions and we so often find incidental advantages attached to them, that we almost take a national pride in anomalies. But in Ireland the Church Establishment is not merely a statistical anomaly. There is an antipathy of the strongest kind between Irish Protestantism and Irish Popery. The Establishment is associated in the minds of the people with an ascendancy against which they had formerly good reason to cherish resentment. The oppression exercised by the English Government towards the native Irish, and often in maintaining the claims of the Anglican Church, was for many generations so steady and relentless, that it might well awaken a desire in the children of the oppressors to make some reparation to the children of the oppressed. Happily, positive oppression has now ceased, and no one wishes to see it renewed. Happily also, there is a general testimony to the respectability and kindly feeling and social usefulness of the Protestant clergy. But there remains this Establishment, built upon the assumption that Ireland was and should be made to be a Protestant country—an assumption to which facts offer as obstinate a denial as ever. Would it not be the next natural step in the policy of equal justice and conciliation, to withdraw the unsupported pretensions of our English religion, and to pay the homage of public and respectful recognition to the religion which the Irish themselves love?

Suppose that we, any of us, were acting on behalf of the legislature of this country, and were dealing face to face with representatives of Irish Roman Catholics: suppose that, in the better spirit of modern government, we wished to make friends with them, and to justify our policy in their eyes; suppose that we expostulated with them, and said: "Why do you continue to be disaffected to the Imperial rule, and to regard your connexion with England as a misfortune? We wish to act justly by you, and we have the power to confer great benefits upon you; the union between England and Ireland is not to be kept up for the sake of England only; why should you not join yourselves to us as heartily as the inhabitants of Scotland have done?" —and suppose that they replied: "It is not very easy to get over our old grudge; there are some things in your policy still which do not suit us; for example, we feel aggrieved by the fact that a Church Establishment is kept up for the benefit of the few and the strong, and that the State deliberately shuts its eyes to our religion." How should we feel? Could we give them an answer which we are sure in our consciences ought to satisfy them? I do not say that any obligation lies upon us to give to the Irish what they would like to have. That is not the point. The question is whether we could give them such an account of the Protestant Establishment,—not as *would* satisfy them,—but as we think, if they were reasonable men, *ought to* satisfy them.

Nor do I assert that such an account could not be given them. But I do urge that this is a responsibility which we are bound to recognize; the responsibility of dealing in a fair and reasonable and conciliatory spirit with the Roman Catholics who constitute the bulk of the Irish population. Whatever conclusion we may arrive at, no one is warranted in putting out of his thoughts this consideration—What does justice to our Roman Catholic fellow-subjects require at our hands?

There is always a danger that the claims of *religion* may be set against the claims of *justice*. In the present case, sympathy with members of the same Church may seem to make our duty and honour consist in coming to their aid, and guarding them from any humiliation and injury with which they may be threatened. And on the other hand, some may feel that if they could forget that they are members of the reformed Church of England and Ireland, and remember only that they are citizens of the British Empire, a sense of equity might induce them to be tender towards the self-respect of their Roman Catholic fellow-subjects. Now when religion and justice seem to come into competition, what is our duty? I answer earnestly and without hesitation: We ought *always* to lean to the side of *justice*. There are two simple reasons for thus deciding. One is, that it is a constant and deadly temptation to religious persons to be indifferent to mere secular justice. Another is, that according to all Bible teaching we please God better by being righteous or equitable, and respectful to the consciences of our fellow-men, than by any strictly religious services. The prophets are full of testimonies to this effect. Men thought to please God by sacrifices, by fastings, by observance of days—in a word, by religion. They were told that these things, offered by men who did not seek to be righteous, were actually an abomination to the Lord. The voice of the prophets is summed up in these words: "Wherewith shall I come before the Lord, and bow myself before the high God? Shall I come before him with burnt-offerings, with calves of a year old? Will the Lord be pleased with thousands of rams, or with ten thousands of rivers of oil?...He hath shewed thee, O man, what is good: and what doth the Lord require of thee, but to do justly, and to love mercy, and to walk humbly with thy God?" In the New Testament, the whole life of Christ teaches the same truth even more powerfully than his words. He took the side of the irreligious, because they were poor and scorned and oppressed, against the religious, because they were hard and haughty. If we follow Christ, we must confess that to be just and merciful and humble is a better thing than to be scrupulous in our creed and in our acts of worship. First the former, and then the latter; first righteousness, then religion. "If thou bring thy gift to the altar, and there rememberest that thy brother hath ought against thee, leave there thy gift before the altar, and go thy way; first be reconciled to thy brother, and then come and offer thy gift."

This sacred duty, of earnestly seeking to do justly, is what I principally desire, dear brethren, to commend to you this morning. This is the lesson which more than any other seems to belong to the subject which we have been considering. My own opinion on the political question, as you would infer it to some extent from what I have said, it may be convenient to state explicitly. If I give it frankly, I hope it is with sincere respect for those who may differ from me, and without any desire to take an advantage of them. To me it does not seem compatible with an equitable and considerate policy towards Ireland, that the Established Church should retain its present ascendancy there. If we sympathise, as we ought to do, with our Irish fellow-Churchmen, it must indeed be painful to us to take away their privileges, and to inflict on them what must look like a humiliation before their opponents and before the world. But our sympathies are not due to our co-religionists alone. And to perform an act of reparation is never really a humiliation. It will be good for our religion in the long run that we should endeavour at any sacrifice "to do justly, and to love mercy, and to walk humbly with God."

There are more ways than one in which we might attempt to carry out a fair and conciliatory policy towards the native Irish. The plan which has for the present gained the support of the House of Commons is that of disestablishing the Anglican Church, and disendowing religion generally in Ireland. I should much prefer that a different plan should be tried. I differ entirely from those who think it is a good thing in itself that all bonds between the State and religion should as far as possible be severed. I am convinced on the contrary that it is good for the State and for religion that the Government and the religion of a country should be united by as many ties as possible. Personally, therefore, I go with those who would have endeavoured to arrange that, instead of *dis*establishment, there should be more establishment, and that the Imperial Government should enter into just and reasonable relations with Roman

Catholics as well as Protestants, with Presbyterians as well as Anglicans.

But I repeat once more, in conclusion, that my purpose this morning is not to advocate an opinion. It is to set before you the great divine principle of righteousness or equity. In private and in public dealings, let us labour earnestly to be just towards all men. Perhaps in this matter our private is a little in advance of our public morality. We should all feel it to be a shame to take advantage of position to be hard upon a weaker person. Let us remember that a strong class ought equally to be ashamed of being hard upon a weaker class or a weaker race. We count it a credit to acknowledge a wrong and to make reparation if we have injured an individual. Let us remember that a nation may seek and may gain honour by the same magnanimity. If we love our country, if we love our Church, let us do our part that both may have the greatness of acting in the generous self-denying spirit of Christ; let us exercise ourselves that both in Church and in State we may "do justly, and love mercy, and walk humbly with our God."

THE MORALITY OF THE LORD'S SUPPER.

DISCOURSE I.

THE EUCHARIST.*

In a recent volume of Essays, written to illustrate the political doctrines of the French philosopher M. Comte, one of the writers expresses his anticipation of the approaching downfall of Christianity in the following words: "Whatever a clergy may think, no religious organization can long hold its ground in popular esteem when confronted by a loftier morality than its own†." It is the Christian morality that is the less lofty. If it were only urged that the morality which it is the business of the clergy to teach is in some points defective or eccentric, such an opinion would not be unprecedented. But it is a new thing that the Christian Faith should be condemned on account of the lower tone of its morality,—that the advocates of a system which claims to be absolutely universal, and which absolutely excludes and suppresses all belief in anything more Divine than the human race, should disdain to use the common language of unbelief, and instead of saying, "The Christian

* This and the two following Sermons were preached before the University of Cambridge.

† *Essays on International Policy*, pp. 220, 221.

morality is beautiful and will live, but the Christian dogmas are contrary to reason and must perish," should confront Christianity with the boast, "The higher morality must prevail, and therefore the Christian Church is doomed." It is superfluous to repudiate in the name of the clergy the imputation that they are conscious of the inferiority of the Christian morality, and are depending upon some other force for the support of their creed. But it is awakening and useful to know that taunts like these have been addressed to us, and that Christians are challenged to let their faith be tried by the excellence of its proper morality.

It is a more familiar and less startling assertion, that the Christian morality is not so vitally attached to the Christian creed that, if the creed is abandoned, the morality must wither. We may often see it earnestly and scientifically maintained, that an ethical system practically identical with the Christian law of duty may be based upon the experience of what promotes the happiness of mankind, and that the sense of what is good for mankind will be found an adequate motive without any other for the observance of this system.

At the same time that systems of morality are thus offered to us, which own no allegiance whatever to a belief in Christ or in God, and which profess to be either loftier in tone or in more exact accordance with facts than Christian morality, there is a well-known tendency now prevailing to cultivate in the Church a religion more mystical, making its appeal more exclusively to the peculiar religious and devotional instincts, and in this sense less moral, less rational, than our English religion has commonly professed to be.

To all who feel the gravity of the divorce so threatened from both sides between devotional religion and every-day morality,—to those especially who retain the old Christian and English persuasion, that our faith in Christ is still the deepest and surest basis of a universal morality, and that a religion which does not willingly accept the moral life of men in general as its proper sphere and criterion is likely to become a superstition, with all the baneful influences which superstition has proved itself powerful to exert,—I venture to commend the subject on which I am about to enter in these discourses. I ask you to reflect upon the *moral aspects of the Sacrament of the Lord's Supper*. In that Sacrament we have a rite which contains by universal agreement the very heart of our ritual religion. It is our most honoured ordinance; it holds the key of all our secrets. It is the crowning act of our worship throughout Christendom, everywhere performed with most reverence, looked forward to with most awe, wearing to the common mind the most sacred investiture of associations. Those who are now seeking to revive amongst us a disused policy of working upon the religious affections make it their chief aim to heighten the mystery and solemnity of this rite. Let us inquire then what natural connexions there are between this the most religious act of our religion and the principles of universal human life. And let us be guided in our inquiry by three names applied to this Sacrament, Eucharist, Sacrifice, and Communion.

The first of these names, the Eucharist, a name scarcely familiar to the childhood of the present generation, has been brought into use of late years by those who have desired that this Sacrament should be regarded with a deeper awe. It is a venerable ecclesiastical name; but, if its significance be considered, it is one which might be accepted without distaste by the most ultra-Protestant. What Christian is there, even amongst Puritans or Rationalists, who would not gladly call the celebration of the Lord's Supper an act of Thanksgiving? In its most unmystical character as a bare commemoration, this Sacrament cannot be anything less than our great Thanksgiving Service. But those to whom the Sacrament is mystical and awful are not inconsistent in bearing witness that the highest possible act of human worship is well designated a Thanksgiving. They are not betraying their principle when they delight to call our participation in the Body and Blood of Christ the Holy Thanksgiving. They may be understood to affirm in this way that in Christian thankfulness there is a mystery which passes all understanding. And assuredly, whether the most sacred language of the Communion Office be considered, or the doctrine of the Apostles as to the inner nature of the Christian life, the name of the Eucharist will commend itself as one of peculiar dignity and significance.

Can any one who thinks what words mean read without wonder that saying of St Paul's, "Giving thanks always for all things unto God and the Father in the name of our Lord Jesus Christ"? He has been speaking of the high privileges of Christians, bidding his readers think of themselves as God's beloved children and as enlightened with the Divine light of Christ, and he claims that their life should be a life of joy, of inspiration, of thankfulness. "Be filled with the Spirit; speaking to yourselves in psalms and hymns and spiritual songs, singing and making melody in your heart to the Lord, giving thanks always for all things unto God and the Father in the name of our Lord Jesus Christ." Other and various affections will be excited by varying circumstances; but throughout all circumstances alike the basis of the Christian life should be eucharistical. To what a depth in the human heart must the spirit of thankfulness reach, to make such a condition possible! The writings of St Paul are everywhere full of evidences that he, for one, recognized the law of abiding thankfulness as practically binding upon himself and his fellow-Christians. Thus he says to the Thessalonians, "Rejoice evermore: pray without ceasing: *in everything give thanks; for this is the will of God* in Christ Jesus concerning you." And there is a remarkable passage (2 Cor. viii. ix.) in which

St Paul lingers over the double subject of grace and gratitude, ringing changes in his characteristic manner upon the word χάρις in its various senses of favour, bounty, and thankfulness, and winds up with what may possibly be a primitive liturgical formula, "Thanks be to God for his unspeakable gift!"—an utterance not the less impressive as a testimony to the law of thankfulness, because it is uncertain whether by that gift we are to understand God's grace, or the Gospel, or the Saviour himself, the Son whom the Father gave for the redemption of mankind.

In the Holy Eucharist this principle of thankfulness has had from the first its peculiar witness and expression. The Jewish Passover to which it succeeded was itself a Eucharist. When Jesus kept it for the last time with his disciples, he gave thanks, or blessed, before the distribution of the bread, and again before the giving of the cup. In so doing he was observing the common custom, according to which the Paschal feast was celebrated with the chanting of the special Eucharistic Psalms, and every act of it accompanied by some formula of thanksgiving. The thankfulness of the Paschal feast was handed on to the Lord's Supper of the Christian Church, only gaining depth and intensity from the new occasions of thankfulness which were found in the broken Body and the poured-out Blood. The Christians delighted to call their most solemn rite the Εὐχαριστία or the Εὐλογία, the Thanksgiving, or the Blessing. These titles were not regarded as accidental names, but as giving welcome expression to the true significance and spirit of the ordinance. Thus St Chrysostom, whilst he speaks of the sacramental celebrations as "awful mysteries, fraught with much salvation," explains that the service is called "the Thanksgiving, because it is a remembrance of many benefits, and shews forth the crowning act of God's regard, and prepares us to be perpetually thankful*." In exact harmony with these words is the Exhortation addressed by the Priest in our English office to those who are about to communicate. "*Above all things,*" he is bidden to say, "ye must give most humble and hearty *thanks* to God." "To the end that we should alway remember the exceeding great love of our Master and only Saviour Jesus Christ thus dying for us, and the innumerable benefits which by his precious bloodshedding he hath obtained to us; he hath instituted and ordained holy mysteries, as pledges of his love, and for a continual remembrance of his death, to our great and endless comfort. To him therefore, with the Father and the Holy Ghost, let us give, as we are most bounden, continual thanks." And, as the service proceeds, it is evidently the chief aim of the forms of this office to animate to the very utmost the Eucharistical spirit. The redeeming love of the Father, the tenderness of Christ, the assured forgiveness of God, are declared in comfortable words; the duty and reasonableness of being

* Chrysostom, *Hom. in Matth.* xxv. (Matth. vii. 28).

thankful are urged; and the worshippers are drawn on by the inspiring contagion of example and voice, and as it were compelled to give thanks. The Priest says "Lift up your hearts," and the people answer "We lift them up unto the Lord;" again he calls on them, "Let us give thanks unto our Lord God," and again they assent, "It is meet and right so to do;" and then he turns to the Lord's table, and speaking to God in the name of the people confesses, "It is very meet, right, and our bounden duty, that we should at all times and in all places give thanks unto thee, O Lord, Holy Father, Almighty, Everlasting God;" and so begins to lead that greatest choral thanksgiving of the Universal Church, "Therefore with angels and archangels, and with all the company of heaven, we laud and magnify thy glorious name; evermore praising thee, and saying, Holy, holy, holy, Lord God of hosts, heaven and earth are full of thy glory: Glory be to thee, O Lord most high." When the Bread is given, and again when the Cup is given, the communicant is bidden to be thankful; the Prayer which follows the reception, in either of its alternative forms, begins with thanksgiving, and the office concludes with the *Gloria in excelsis*, in which the Eucharistical spirit seems to strive with the inadequacy of human words in the utterance of gratitude and praise.

Whilst we observe so manifest a desire to make the Holy Eucharist really a Eucharist, we see also that the office itself repeatedly declares that the thankfulness of the Christian cannot be limited to a service, but must be diffused through the whole life. At all times and in all places it is our duty to give thanks. The Eucharist bears witness to this duty in its fulness. The benefits for which we give thanks are not temporary or local. He whom we thank is one to whom we may have access whenever and wherever we will. Our gratitude to God rests upon a sense of his goodness to us, joined with the consciousness of our own unworthiness. God is good to us: but *how* good is he? The Holy Eucharist replies, that God *so* loved us as to give his Son in our flesh and blood to die for us, and this, whilst we were yet sinners. No other account of God's love can equal this measure of it; and the Sacrament of the Eucharist helps us against our own carelessness and forgetfulness to realize it. But if we ask, *When* is God good to us?—the Eucharistic answer is, *Always*. He to whom we give thanks for the gift of his Son is the Eternal Maker, the Ruler of the world and of our destinies. We are his creatures; we can assert no independence in his sight. "What hast thou which thou didst not receive?" The relation between God and men revealed to us in Christ,—that spiritual sonship to which we cannot be conformed without spiritual discipline,—enables us to understand how God, the giver of all pleasant things, may be still good in withholding or taking away pleasant things. And thus the true disciple of the Eucharist learns a thankfulness which confesses God's greatest benefit only that it may recognize all things as benefits. Contemplating the glory of the Cross, he beholds a glory of which heaven and earth are full. Thankfulness for Christ is as a reservoir from which all the fields of human life are watered.

Has thankfulness to God, supposing that it thus belongs to the atmosphere of the Lord's Supper, any moral value in human life?

I do not ask the question merely for the purposes of controversy. At the same time let it be remembered that those who frame any complete scheme of duty or morality without taking account of God have no place for this thankfulness in their estimate of moral forces. But those who affirm most strongly our dependence upon God may find benefit, I hope, from a recollection of some of the salutary influences which human life owes to the spirit of thankfulness.

1. Let me name first the power of thankfulness to make the thankful person *happy*. Thankfulness is inseparably associated with joy; all the terms of gladness and delight lend themselves naturally to thanksgiving. "O praise the Lord; for it is a good thing to sing praises unto our God, yea, a joyful and pleasant thing it is to be thankful." This is a truth of nature, capable of infinite illustration, but so certainly commending itself as to need none. What I would especially ask you to think of is the immense power which belongs to thankfulness, as the true "spirit of delight," if only it become deep and earnest enough, to diffuse and

secure happiness amongst men. Make all men thankful, and you have made the world a happy world. The gratitude which is occasional and temporary will easily evaporate indeed in superficial emotions. But imagine such thankfulness as St Paul believed in, and such as the Eucharist hallows, to be lodged in a man's heart; who can doubt the power of it? The only question must be whether to a man with open eyes such a thankfulness is possible; and I do not speak without remembering how much there is to persuade us that it is only a dream. No doubt the perfect Christian thankfulness is ideal, and has never been more than imperfectly realized; but it has surely proved itself in the experience of the truest and best of men, and daily proves itself, to be no mere fiction of an excited brain. Men *have* given God thanks with a sincere inward joy out of fires and dungeons of tribulation. We cannot doubt "that some have striven Achieving calm, to whom was given The joy that mixes man with heaven:" and we may claim to be reasonable and practical, when we recognize in thankfulness, according to its depth and intensity, a power to make men happy with a happiness which has no drawback. Who can point to a higher or sweeter or more enviable bliss than that which may be seen to radiate from the face of a sufferer, who has learnt to trust in God's love with an unreserved faith and to give thanks even for afflictions?

2. Thankfulness to God is also a genial,

kindly, social feeling. There is indeed a bastard thankfulness which tends to isolation and selfishness, that of the Pharisee who said with himself, "God, I thank thee that I am not as other men are." But the fault of this is simply that it is not thankfulness. It is self-complacency, borrowing the mere form and phrase of thanksgiving. True thankfulness is sure to postpone and depreciate self; and it therefore tends proportionably to promote good feeling and kindly intercourse amongst men. For that which mars fellowship is the assertion of self; it is vanity, jealousy, covetousness, or some other form of self-love. You see a man with whom you cannot hope to get on pleasantly; he may seem hard, or exacting, or irritable, or absorbed in his own schemes, or brooding over his own feelings; but he will certainly not be one in whom the Eucharistic disposition predominates. If vulgarity repels, there is nothing more essentially opposed to vulgarity that a pure and deep thankfulness. We call the benevolent instincts social; but there are many to whom the companionship of a simply thankful person would be more attractive than that of one endowed with an obvious and patent benevolence. We have but to name the synonymous forms of grace, gracious, graciousness, and we read in the common language of mankind a testimony to the power of thankfulness to make men agreeable to one another and to render their mutual intercourse delightful.

3. Again, the thankful spirit guides and encourages *purity*.

It does so, because it takes everything *as a gift from God*. It grasps at nothing; it respects with a natural submission the ordinances of the Creator. Whenever "this is forbidden" is marked upon any indulgence within a man's reach, the thankful spirit willingly renounces it, knowing no such thing as a sense of injury in matters between God and the soul, believing that God in commanding us to abstain is doing us no less a benefit than if he bade us receive, and turning with simplicity and contentment to the enjoyment of what he gives.

St Paul shews incidently, in more than one place, with what confidence he was accustomed to depend on the principle of thankfulness to God as a moral safeguard. "The earth is the Lord's," he says, "and the fulness thereof." Nothing, therefore, is to be shunned or dreaded as in itself evil; the Christian is free to take or not as it may be advantageous for himself and his brethren. "For," argues St Paul, "if I partake with thankfulness, why am I evil spoken of for that for which I give thanks?" He seems to assume that a man cannot well be doing wrong if in eating or in not eating he is thankful to God and keeps his glory in view. And again he warns Timothy against those who forbid to marry and command to abstain from meats, "which God hath created to be received with thanksgiving by them who believe and know the truth. For every creature of God is good, and nothing to be refused, if it be received with thanksgiving." St Paul did not mean, of course, that laws and ordinances were abolished for the Christian, and that he could make any indulgence lawful by adding to it an act of thanksgiving. He assumed that the spirit of thankfulness would dispose a man to study and inquire what the will of the Lord is, and compel him to obey that will cheerfully when he knows it. And might he not make that assumption safely? Let a man try to be thankful for something which he knows in his conscience to be illegitimate, for dissipation which wastes his time and weakens his moral if not his bodily strength, for an advantage won unfairly at the expense of a neighbour, for increase of wealth to which he is selling his soul, even for a thing which is innocent except that he cares too much about it,—and he will learn by the contradiction which will rise within him what a spear of Ithuriel he possesses in thankfulness, and how impossible it is for the thankful heart to be other than temperate and pure.

4. And whilst we might be guarded from evil as that which is displeasing to God, so we might be made more receptive and appreciative towards all good, by the same temper of thankfulness to the gracious and bountiful Father. Much is lost,—who can say how much?—especially of the finest and most spiritual influences which move in the atmosphere of the world, through the indifference and insensibility of selfish natures. It is one of the happy effects of a continual thankfulness, that it opens the character, like a warm and genial climate,

and makes it tenderer and more susceptible to such influences. If we are daily thanking God for the gift, above all, of his Son, and of the Spirit of his Son, we shall be so turned to what is most Divine, that all that is God-like, all that is loving and healthful and pure, will be welcome to us and give us pleasure. Our sympathies will be refined, and we shall be the richer, and the world will be the richer, through our thankfulness.

5. Again, it is worth while to observe briefly the power which thankfulness has to sustain and adjust other virtues. Let us take two instances.

Humility and a just self-esteem have some appearance of being contradictory the one to the other. It is a Christian excellence to be humble: "in lowliness of mind," says the Apostle, "let each esteem other better than themselves." But truth would have a man think of himself as neither better nor worse than he is; and we know how advantageous a noble pride is in preserving men from what is mean and unworthy. Now the thankful Christian says, "By the grace of God I am what I am;" but he can also add, "By my own fault I am what I am." It will be his continual desire to refer all that is good in him to God, and therefore on fitting occasions to do justice to it, and to refer all that is unworthy in him to himself, and therefore always to humble himself on account of it. Thus it is quite possible for a man to think both highly and lowly concerning himself: pride and humility are both justified by thankfulness.

Liberality in the use of money finds a great help in thankfulness. The lines of our childhood "Not more than others I deserve, But God has given me more," express a conviction which can hardly fail to make and keep a man liberal. Can I thank God, as one whom God has blessed beyond any deservings of his own, for what he has given me, and not be ready—more ready than those whose only view of their possessions is that they have acquired or inherited them—to do whatever may be best with my money for the good of my neighbours and my brethren? And there will be a *grace* (the word is again a testimony) in the liberality of a thankful person, which is less likely to adorn and sweeten that of a calculating benevolence.

6. Lastly, the principle of thankfulness has a marked value in the sphere of the political relations of human societies.

It is a familiar practice of rulers and statesmen to appoint Days of Thanksgiving for events which the people recognize as good for the land. This is done in countries which have not the convenience of a single State Church, as well as in our own and in the old Roman Catholic countries. There are cases in which, as in Switzerland, the existing settlement of the constitution is commemorated by a yearly Thanksgiving-Sunday. No doubt the religious feelings of the population have demanded this kind of observance; but statesmen from their point of view have seen its utility. It is impossible to imagine a more valuable political sentiment in a country than that of a reverent thankfulness to God for all that is good in its history and constitution. To cling to what has come down from the past with a blind superstition; to treat with a careless levity historical institutions, as if any generation could unmake and make at will its own political system:—each of these habits is feared and deprecated by all wise citizens. We are armed against both, when we thank God under whose good Providence our fathers lived and wrought, and to whose present help and guidance we ourselves may equally appeal. But the most immediate and valued effect of national thanksgivings is to bind the population together in one brotherly feeling. By the joy of common thankfulness families and classes are spiritually welded together; a love for the common inheritance, fellow-feeling amongst all who share it, are naturally fostered. The words of the Hebrew patriot can yet find an echo in all loyal hearts, "Jerusalem is built as a city that is at unity in itself. For thither the tribes go up, even the tribes of the Lord, to testify unto Israel, to give thanks unto the name of the Lord."

These are some of the illustrations which have occurred to me as shewing the moral value of the Eucharistical principle in human life. You may have hardly needed them to deepen your conviction that those who banish thankfulness to God by recognizing no God to be thanked, are expelling the very juice and sap from morality, and robbing life of some of its finest bloom. But we all have abundant need to be reminded how much we lose by not conforming ourselves to the spirit of our holiest mysteries. The Eucharist, we have seen, does not separate itself from secular life. It demands for its own celebration a feeling which can only be brought to it by those who are habitually thankful; it seeks to raise that feeling to its highest power, and to send it pulsing again through our daily experience. Our whole worship, rightly understood, is in harmony with the service in which it culminates, and would spread and preserve the same influence. All our prayers are to be accompanied with thanksgiving,—nay, must rest on thanksgiving as their basis. For thankfulness, whilst it can make no claim to be exempt from the logical difficulties which are more usually urged against prayer, is deeper than prayer. Our hope that God will hear us depends on what God has done for us. "He that spared not his own Son, but delivered him up for us all,—how shall he not with him also freely give us all things?" Day by day, Sunday after Sunday, we utter words of gratitude and praise for all that God has done for us. Are we not unfaithful Christians, untrue to the privileges of our creed and our worship, in that we do not carry about with us hearts more steadfastly thankful? We are encompassed,—you that are yet living here under the shadow of ancient learning and piety, no less, assuredly, than those of us whose lot is cast elsewhere,—by blessings old and new. These will become dearer and more helpful to us as we thank God for them all,

> From the gift looking to the Giver,
> And from the cistern to the River,
> And from the finite to Infinity,
> And from man's dust to God's Divinity.

DISCOURSE II.

SACRIFICE.

In speaking of the word *Sacrifice* as one of the titles of the Lord's Supper, we encounter a difficulty which did not present itself to us in considering the significance of the word Eucharist. A large proportion of English Christians are not indeed in the habit of using the former term, the Holy Eucharist, when they have occasion to mention this Sacrament. But this is simply a matter of custom. If the meaning of the word is borne in mind, it cannot possibly be regarded by any Christian as objectionable on doctrinal grounds that the Lord's Supper should be designated as our Thanksgiving-Service. *The Holy Sacrifice* is not a title that would be accepted with equal acquiescence. I am aware that many would repudiate and condemn it as implying doctrine which our own Church has disclaimed. But it cannot be denied that in using our Communion Office we find a prominent place given to the idea and the name of sacrifice. And, in speaking of the connexion which properly subsists between the most sacred Christian ordinance and common morality, I prefer to contemplate this Sacrament from the point of view of those to whom it is most awful and furthest removed from the associations and conditions of ordinary life: as on the other hand it belongs to my purpose to keep in view the secular systems of morality in which a theory of human virtue is constructed without taking any account of God. And the word Sacrifice seems to me peculiarly valuable and instructive, as linking the deepest faith and highest worship of the Christian with the principle of every-day duty.

This word may be claimed, no doubt, by Roman Catholics and by those who approximate closely to Roman Catholics as fitly expressing what takes place according to their belief when the Sacrament of the Lord's Supper is celebrated. They have, they would say, at their altar the two essential elements of a sacrifice—the *hostia* or victim, and the sacrificing priest. To the inquiry "Where is the lamb for a burnt-offering?" it is answered that the priest has the power to call down the Lamb of God from heaven, and that after the act of consecration the Lord Jesus Christ is present as a sacrificial victim under the outward form of bread, or of bread and wine. But such a sacrifice is professedly of the nature of a *fleshly* sacrifice; this is its boast. And if we were able to accept those assertions, it would still be open to us, and surely incumbent on us as Christians, to inquire what is the essentially *spiritual* sacrifice of which that in the flesh is the instrument or exponent. All sacrifices are acceptable to God just in proportion as they are spiritual. The spirit is to beware, it is true, of repudiating the flesh as evil or insignificant; but the spirit is always higher than the flesh, even were it the flesh of the Son of God himself.

It is worth while, perhaps, to apply this observation at the present time to all theories as to the mode of the Real Presence, or, as it is sometimes called, the Real Objective Presence, of Christ in the celebration of the Lord's Supper. I do not wish to advocate or to oppose any definition upon this subject. It is far easier to contend with words about the nature of that Presence, than to be sure that we understand either our own words or those of our opponents. And the line of thought which I have suggested may be followed, I hope, by Christians who are not all willing to use the same language on the controverted question of the Real Presence. But all who hold any opinions whatever as to the relation between the Body and Blood of Christ and the consecrated elements may be reminded with advantage of what all must equally admit,—I mean, the natural superiority of that which is spiritual over that which is corporeal.

It is often assumed that in proportion as men approximate in opinion to the doctrine of the Church of Rome, called Transubstantiation, in that proportion the Presence in the Sacrament becomes more truly awful. And this is taken for granted on both sides; it is conceded as well as claimed.

"If it were only true," it is said, "that Christ is really present on the altar, no homage could possibly be too profound for that Divine Presence, no dress could be too rich or ornaments too costly for those who approach it, no prostrations before it too humble." The awful effect of the corporeal or quasi-corporeal presence is not the matter commonly disputed, nor the kind of reverence it would demand; one side affirms, "Christ *is* thus present," the other side replies, "He is not, or not in the awful manner you suppose." But take the extreme case, as including all other opinions that in any degree approach it; suppose all that the most advanced Romanist has ever put forward as to the Bodily Presence of Christ in the Sacrament to be true. Is Christ infinitely more worthy of our reverence when presented to us under some bodily form, than when he is not under a form of which our senses can take cognizance?

The awfulness and dignity of the Sacramental host can hardly be greater than would belong to the visible human form of Jesus Christ, such as the eyes of the Apostles saw and their hands handled at Jerusalem or in Galilee. If the Lord Jesus were thus to manifest himself amongst us, who would turn from that form to worship with a deeper reverence the bread or the wafer of the Sacrament? But we do not gather from the New Testament that the Christ visible in the flesh upon the earth was worshipped by his disciples with a more adoring homage than the Christ at the

Father's right hand in heaven. The Apostles did not feel after the day of Pentecost that their God was lost to them. It is undeniable, on the contrary, that they then worshipped Christ with a more assured faith, that they rejoiced in him with a deeper joy, than when he had been going in and out amongst them. Their Master had prepared them for this advance in Spiritual apprehension. He told them that he must depart in order that the Spirit might come to them, and that when the Spirit came he would be with them again in a far more satisfying manner. "I will not leave you bereaved, I will come to you. Yet a little while, and the world seeth me no more; but ye see me: because I live, ye shall live also. At that day ye shall know that I am in my Father, and ye in me, and I in you." The Apostles undoubtedly believed that these promises were fulfilled; it was their settled conviction that the Spirit had infinitely more power in enabling them to have fellowship with Christ than any bodily presence.

It may be said that what makes the Bodily Presence in the Sacrament so much more awful than Christ's spiritual presence is that it is brought to the altar by a miracle. But a miracle is treated by our Lord himself as a condescension to the senses, which it is not creditable to faith to require; and a miracle which, like Transubstantiation, makes no appeal to the senses is without even that lower virtue of a miracle. If the Apostles would have felt that they were descending to a lower spiritual level in craving for the renewed presence of Jesus as he had been before his death, it is hardly likely that their deepest reverence would have been stirred by seeing him in bodily presence under the form of a wafer.

Whether therefore the Bread and the Wine are miraculously changed in any manner or degree into the Body and Blood of Christ, or are made to represent the Body and the Blood without any alteration of their substance, it is equally important that the worshippers should not make more of the flesh than of the spirit, and that they should strive to realize above all in the Spirit the spiritual presence of God. Christ local upon the altar or in the priest's hand is not so awful, not so essentially Divine, as Christ in us. If our spirits are to acknowledge their true Lord and deliverer, they must look, not into the priest's hand, but upwards to the eternal throne. If they are to be penetrated by the deepest and most sanctifying awe, they must learn something of the meaning of those words, "At that day ye shall know that I am in my Father, and ye in me, and I in you."

This truth should especially be borne in mind when we are considering the moral aspect of the Lord's Supper in the light of the idea of Sacrifice. For Sacrifice, as I have said, can only be acceptable to God in so far as it is spiritual. It makes no difference whether the oblation be of an animal's life, or of devotion and good works; what God regards is always the spirit that offers it. The

Sacrifice of the Son of God was infinitely precious because he offered himself through the Eternal Spirit to the Father.

I have referred to the repugnance felt by many in our own Church to the use of the word Sacrifice as a title of the Lord's Supper. This repugnance has much to justify it, but we find less reason for cherishing it when we perceive how customary it was amongst the early Fathers of the Church to call the Lord's Supper a Sacrifice, before the doctrine of Transubstantiation was received, and without implying anything like that doctrine. There are two words continually associated with sacrifice in their writings; one of them is "remembrance," the other is "rational," the former taken from our Lord's saying, "Do this in remembrance of me," the latter from St Paul's expression (Romans xii. 1), "Which is your reasonable or rational service." Thus the Lord's Supper is called "the remembrance of the sacrifice once offered;" it is said that Christ "handed down to us *a memory* to offer by way of a sacrifice continually to God*;" and St Chrysostom thus corrects himself, "Our sacrifice is one; we do not vary it, but always offer the same, *or rather*, we celebrate a *remembrance* of a sacrifice †." And that epithet of St Paul's, rational, λογική, is very commonly joined with sacrifice, implying that the sacrifice or worship is an act of the mind or understanding. And the same idea is conveyed by

---
* Eusebius, *Demonst. Evang.* 1. 10.
† Chrysostom, *Hom. in Heb.* XVII. (Heb. ix. 25)

similar terms, which describe the Christian sacrifice as not corporeal but belonging to the region of the thoughts and the affections. Let me quote two sentences in which this idea is expressed: "We offer our own souls in sacrifice, and present them to God, by dying to the world and to a fleshly mind*." "Our victim is above, our priest above, our sacrifice above. Therefore let us offer such sacrifices as can be presented on that altar †."

In accordance with this venerable language, we observe that the idea of sacrifice enters in a two-fold manner into the celebration of the Lord's Supper. (1) We remember and plead and as it were present anew the Sacrifice of Christ once made for men, (2) and we come to offer sacrifices of our own.

The Sacrifice of Christ was consummated in his death, by the breaking of his body and the shedding of his blood. It was precisely this that the Sacrament was instituted to set forth. Jesus said "Do this in remembrance of me; in remembrance of me as giving my body and pouring out my blood for you." The whole sacramental ceremony has reference to this death of Christ. When we call Christ's death a Sacrifice, we mean that he offered himself through death to the Father. The Prayer of Consecration in our Office begins by pleading this Sacrifice. It appeals to the Father as having himself originated the Sacrifice, and calls upon him by his own tender mercy

---

* Cyril. Alex. *de Adorat.* XI. p. 402.
† Chrysostom, *Hom. in Heb.* XI. (Heb. vi. 13).

shewn in this act. "Almighty God, our heavenly Father, who of thy tender mercy didst give thine only Son Jesus Christ to suffer death upon the Cross for our redemption; who made there by his one oblation of himself once offered a full, perfect, and sufficient sacrifice, oblation, and satisfaction, for the sins of the whole world;...hear us, O merciful Father, we most humbly beseech thee."—A very earnest expression of what was taught by our Lord and by his Apostles concerning his Sacrifice. It was the Father who sent the Son to die for us, who purchased to himself a universal Church by the precious blood of his dear Son. The Son surrendered himself willingly to the Father's will. "Lo, I come,"—this was the principle of his sacrifice,—"to do thy will, O God." His whole life in the flesh therefore was a part of his self-oblation; but the offering culminated, when he gave himself up in the agonies of the Passion and the darkness of death and the grave. This offering, the Church rejoices to believe, was perfect. When the Son, in obedience to the Father's will, had offered himself in human flesh through suffering and death to his Father, nothing further was wanted to open the way completely for humanity to the heart of God. The Father was perfectly well pleased in the Son, who was the head of our sinful race. The Son took upon himself the sins of his brethren, and in his Person human sin was brought into contact with the Divine forgiveness, and was swallowed up by it. We remember in our Sacrament the Offering which was thus perfect and precious; we re-enact in a manner that Sacrifice; we present it by the lifting up of our minds and spirits, as the demonstration of his own love and as the response of the Son's love, to our Father in heaven. The Sacrament of the Body and Blood of Christ was instituted and made perpetual, in order that the redeeming Death of Christ might be thus set continually in reconciling power between God and our sinful souls.

This is, it is plain, an eminently religious rite, full of what it pleases many to call dogma. Has it anything directly to do with the moral activity of human life?—The word Sacrifice has another application in the Sacrament, as we have seen, besides its reference to the Self-oblation of Christ. If Christ gave himself for us, it belongs to us to give ourselves with him. If he opened a way for us to the Father, it is our part to approach God by it. If Christ made himself a Sacrifice, we ought to make ourselves sacrifices.

I have reminded you how the Prayer which precedes the partaking of the Bread and the Wine appeals to the Father in the name of the Divine Sacrifice. Let me quote now a part of the Prayer which follows the communicating: "Here we offer and present unto thee, O Lord, ourselves, our souls and bodies, to be a reasonable, holy, and lively sacrifice unto thee......And although we be unworthy, through our manifold sins, to offer unto thee any sacrifice, yet we beseech thee to accept this our bounden duty and service; not weighing our merits, but pardoning our offences, through Jesus Christ our Lord." It is assumed that we cannot realize the Sacrifice of Christ—that we cannot cry for help to God as the Father who gave his Son and to whom the Son offered himself—that we cannot feed upon his self-oblation—without being drawn to offer ourselves like him to God, in order that his will and nothing else may be done by us. Christ is laid as a foundation, in order that we may build, or be built up, upon it. "To whom coming," says St. Peter, "as unto a living stone, disallowed indeed of men, but chosen of God and precious, ye also, as living stones, are being built up, a spiritual house, an holy priesthood, to offer up spiritual sacrifices, acceptable to God by Jesus Christ." Similarly, St Paul says, "Be ye therefore followers, or imitators, of God, as dear children; and walk in love, as Christ also hath loved us, and hath given himself for us, an offering and a sacrifice to God for a sweet-smelling savour." And again, "I am crucified with Christ; nevertheless I live; yet not I, but Christ liveth in me: and the life which I now live in the flesh I live by the faith of the Son of God, who loved me, and gave himself for me." But it is needless to multiply passages to prove how natural and necessary it seemed to the Apostles that those who believed that Christ had offered himself in their behalf to the Father's will, should consecrate themselves as sacrifices to the same will.

What is the meaning for us of our presenting

ourselves, souls and bodies, as living sacrifices to God? Sacrifice is sometimes spoken of as equivalent to self-denial. It involves self-denial, no doubt, but it is more than equivalent to it. It assumes a living Will, at whose disposal we place ourselves: and the reality and the character of that Will become, when Sacrifice is in question, supremely important. We believe in a God who wills; we believe that he is perfectly good,—just, merciful, true, and that therefore his will chooses all that is good; we believe that the living God, who is all-good, governs the universe and adjusts the place of each one of us in an order of which he is the maker; we believe that God has made his will known in manifesting his Son, and that we may learn its principles in the life of Jesus Christ; we believe that we are intended to discover what God's will is in particular cases by trying to do what is right, and by studying the effect of our actions. We further believe that God loves us, and has called us to sonship in his Son, and desires us to trust in him as children trust in a Father. In this faith we are exhorted to make ourselves sacrifices to God. We are taught to fix our eyes on a Deliverer who has conquered sin and death for us, and has reappeared out of the darkness and mystery of the grave. We have the promise of a Spirit of Sacrifice from above, which is the perfect filial Spirit, the Spirit proceeding from the Father and the Son.

Thus to give ourselves up in the faith of Christians involves an utter subjection and surrender of our own wills. The law of this subjection is as inexorable as those who speak of the danger of such a belief can represent it to be. To the thorough Christian neither his own will nor the wills or opinions of any number of men can count as anything compared with the will of God. He owns it as his duty not to be conformed to this world, but to be transformed by the renewing of his mind, that he may prove by experience what is the good and acceptable and perfect will of God. But, if the character in which he knows God is that of the Father of men and the maker and sustainer of the world's order, if he is continually thanking God for having so loved the world as to give His Son that the world might be saved, if his earnest hope is always for a glory of God which is identified with the well-being of the human race, no sacrifice of himself to the will of God is possible which is not also an offering of himself for the real good of mankind. There is a sentence in which St Paul sums up the life of King David, which may be translated in two different ways. St Paul says, that David fell asleep *after he had served his own generation by the will of God*, or *after he had in his own generation served the will of God*. The conduct described by either translation is in the eye of Christian faith identical. It will make no difference to us whether we propose to serve our generation by the will of God, or to serve the will of God in our generation. We do the best service we can to our fellow-men when we are most obedient to God's will; we please God best when we serve our fellow-men most zealously.

And again, it follows from our Christian premisses that the most unreserved offering up of ourselves to the will of God results not in our slavery but in our emancipation. The service of God, as we thankfully acknowledge, is perfect freedom. To be ruled by self or by the world, this is slavery. To submit willingly, with the concurrence of our knowledge and judgment, to the will of our Maker and Father, or, in other words, to the source of all the order and beauty and happiness of the universe, is to inherit our proper freedom. And therefore Sacrifice to God is to be looked upon, not with dread as a painful necessity, but with joy and hope and longing.

Self-denial is recognized without stint in the prevailing non-theistical systems of morality. It is an ignorant slander to reproach the utilitarian ethics of Mr Mill, for example, or the positivist ethics of M. Comte, with pandering to selfishness. In both these systems benevolence and self-sacrifice are as strongly and sincerely advocated as they can be by Christian moralists. Indeed in both, the rule of duty, as between a man and other men, is hardly distinguishable from the Christian rule. Mr Mill thus protests on behalf of his system: "Let utilitarians never cease to claim the morality of self-devotion as a possession which belongs by as good a right to them, as either to the Stoic or to the Transcendentalist. The utilitarian morality does recognize in human beings the power of sacrificing their own greatest good for the good of others... The happiness which forms the utilitarian standard of what is right in conduct, is not the agent's own happiness, but that of all concerned. As between his own happiness and that of others, utilitarianism requires him to be as strictly impartial as a disinterested and benevolent spectator. In the golden rule of Jesus of Nazareth, we read the complete spirit of the ethics of utility. To do as one would be done by, and to love one's neighbour as oneself, constitute the ideal perfection of utilitarian morality."* M. Comte avoids that adoption of "happiness" as an ultimate standard and quantitative measure of right and wrong which seems to excite an instinctive repugnance in minds trained in the Christian school, and treats the inherent superiority of the benevolent sentiments as a principle determined by the necessary conditions of human progress. He, as is well known, has sought to give to the serving of humanity all the characteristics of a religion, and no one can complain of any coldness or want of enthusiasm in M. Comte's own devotion. A third kind of philosophy, commonly spoken of as Pantheistic, of which M. Renan may be taken as an exponent, holds that "for simple natures absolute devotion is the most exquisite of enjoyments and a kind of want;" that "it is a luxury to man to suffer for anything;"

---

* *Utilitarianism*, pp. 24, 25.

and that "if humanity were raised to ten times its present height, man would be so completely disengaged from selfishness that he would be plunged in a perpetual adoration of the true, the good, and the beautiful, rolling from one ecstasy into another, living and dying in a torrent of pleasure."*

What have we to say then, when we compare the moral teaching of our Christian Sacrament as to sacrifice with the morality of those to whom this Sacrament is obsolete?—Not, certainly, that *we* believe in devotion, and *they* in self-love. But this, I think,—that we believe in a Fatherly Providence, greater than humanity, to which we may offer and entrust ourselves, and in a Divine Head who has gone before us and whom we may follow, and in a Spirit which has a higher and more abiding source than either the clearest conviction or the most exquisite sentiment in ourselves. To us *a Gospel* has been preached, a Gospel which is enshrined for ever in the Sacrament of Christ's Body and Blood. According to our experience, humanity is weak, open to the noblest inspirations, capable of heroic actions, but liable to fall, perpetually tempted by selfishness and cowardice, wanting something stronger than itself to cling to and lean upon. It seems hard upon such a nature to say to a man, "You are bound to sacrifice absolutely and for ever your own highest good if such a sacrifice can produce a greater quantity of good elsewhere." We cannot think it an ignoble instinct to shrink from

* *Les Apôtres,* pp. 380, 381, 385.

loss, ruin, annihilation. We believe that the sacrifice is not less perfect because faith can say, "Father, into thy hands I commend my spirit:" we have no fear of a more refined and disguised form of self-love being encouraged by the exhortation, "Let them that suffer according to the will of God commit the keeping of their souls to him in well-doing, as unto a faithful Creator." We rejoice therefore that there is One who knows us and cares for us and will take charge of us, and that he permits us to dedicate ourselves to him, and to pray to him as our Father that his will may be done in us.

Sacrifice ought to seem *more rational* and easier to the Christian than to the non-Christian. Self-denial indeed, in some ordinary degree, is prescribed by plain reasons to every intelligent being. A child soon learns by experience alone that he must repress the desire and deny himself the pleasure of the moment, if he would avoid a greater pain or gain afterwards a higher pleasure. But self-denial practised for the sake of self may only result in a deeper selfishness. And however philosophers may argue, it must be difficult to persuade a man that he ought to give himself to final ruin, that in what concerns the higher part of his being he ought to incur loss, if by doing so he can confer a more than corresponding benefit on others. But to give oneself to God as a child to a Father, this is reasonable and safe, whatever the surrender may cost. And Christ has taught us that the most complete surrender of ourselves to God is in the long run our greatest safety. In one of His profound paradoxes He has said, "He that saves himself will lose himself: he that loses himself for my sake will save himself." To believe this,—to believe that a man can do nothing better than yield himself utterly to Christ and to God,—has proved a very powerful support to countless sufferers. "Therefore we both labour and suffer reproach, because we trust in the living God, the Saviour of all men." "If suffering comes to me," the Christian will say, "when I am doing God's will, I will accept the suffering contentedly because it is God's will. Nay more, I will take it as an instrument of God's gracious discipline; I will rejoice in it as associating me with the sufferings of Christ." But the sense that God desires us to offer ourselves to him and has himself prepared the sacrifice is not only a solid comfort and support when we are trying to give up self; it is also a great inducement and stimulus to make the effort. If we only realize the sacrifice of the Son of God, how simple and necessary a thing it must seem that we should build ourselves upon it! What a contradiction that we should live to ourselves! We have been bought with a price: surely we must glorify God with the bodies and with the souls which are his. The love of Christ constrains us: for we thus judge, that if one died on behalf of all, then all died; and that he died for all, that they who live should not henceforth live to themselves, but to him who died and rose again for them.

So we are exhorted to reason with ourselves; and so, whenever the mystery of the Cross comes home to us, our consciences must speak within us. Christians who have worshipped at the foot of the Cross have learnt all—may we not say?—that the noblest ethics of the world can teach. But I know not what Christian can help being silenced by a kind of reasonable shame when he reflects upon the average tenor of his own life, and of that of his fellow-Christians in general, and compares it with the morality of those who do not acknowledge Christ. I do not mean that our lives are *less* worthy and unselfish than those of unbelievers, but that they ought to be infinitely more so. We have the Gospel, we have Christ, we have the Holy Spirit, and we persuade ourselves that if these were taken away, motives and hopes, moral energy, the better life, would wither, and we should fall into a careless selfishness. But we find ourselves already selfish, already careless; and I think I cannot be departing from the range of common experience when I assume that we have known others,—whether persons who have had the courageous sincerity openly to reject the faith of their fathers, or persons who whilst still nominally Christian do not profess to be religious,—whose practical goodness has often put us to shame. It must be that such persons are worshipping the Eternal Truth, the Eternal Righteousness and Love, with a truer worship, though not using our names, than many religious Christians, and that they are receiving support and strength for which they give thanks, if not with their lips, yet with their lives. But it is surely our part, learning what we can from such as they and even stimulated by their rivalry, to ask for more of the filial Spirit of Sacrifice. Perhaps we have not resorted enough in humble docility to the Sacrament of Sacrifice; yet we know that the most frequent Communions have no magical power to compel men to give themselves up to God. We need to be as much delivered from hardness and formalism in religion as from indifference to religion. Our wisdom is to blend religion and life together, and in both equally to look up to heaven.

May I venture to add a concluding word, having reference to the characteristic temper of this University? It has often been remarked with satisfaction, that the intellectual atmosphere of Cambridge has been calmer, less agitated by the excitements of new theories of belief or unbelief, than that of other places where young men are living and thinking together, and especially than that of the great sister University. But some have not been able to forget that the advantages of intellectual steadiness and moderation, almost invaluable as they are in a place of education, may be purchased at a very high cost. We know,—at this particular season it is superfluous to remind a Cambridge audience,—how much the great distinctions and almost excessive prizes of academical competition are here thought of, and how eagerly they are pursued. If the most ardent minds of a University, instead of being led by an exceptionally wise and enlightened guidance in the paths of moderation, are rather made indifferent to the thoughts which elsewhere shake mankind by an extreme desire of personal success, this result is not wholly to be rejoiced in. It is better to have some griefs and troubles due to the nobler aspirations, than that thousands of young men should be made partakers of a life dulled by a worldly self-regard. May God give us the good and deliver us from the evil! May he preserve peace and quiet to this University and at the same time inspire its members with a Christian ambition to help his cause forward in the world of their day! The world on its part will owe its best gratitude to students and teachers who, exalted by the old courageous spirit of self-oblation, give themselves heartily to serve their own generation by the will of God.

DISCOURSE III.

COMMUNION.

AMONGST the various titles which have been given to the Sacrament of the Lord's Supper, that which the Prayer-book of the Church of England offers for our ordinary use is *The Holy Communion*. When definition is required, as in the Catechism and in the Articles, the strict name of the Sacrament is *the Lord's Supper*. But elsewhere, as especially in the office for the administration of the Sacrament, it is called the Holy Communion. From the first it has been usual in the Church to apply significant titles, according to preference or custom, to the Lord's Supper. I think that the use of this title in our Prayer-book warrants us in regarding it with a special interest as the chosen Anglican name of the great Sacrament of Christendom.

Every one will remember the place in the New Testament in which this title has its source. But it is worth while to recall the characteristic argument of St Paul, in which the word rendered "communion" serves as a kind of key. One value of the passage is that it shews us how outward visible things may be treated as instruments and witnesses of spiritual things, without any confusing of matter and spirit. St Paul warns the Corinthians (in 1 Cor. x.) to beware of idolatry. And he begs their intelligent consideration of a reason which he gives them, why they should not be careless about joining in the festivities of heathen worship. It is difficult to preserve in an English translation the verbal emphasis of the original; but the connexion of thought may be better indicated by the substitution of some word like *participation* for communion. "The cup of blessing which we bless, is it not a participation in the blood of Christ? The bread which we break, is it not a participation in the body of Christ? For we, being many, are one bread, one body; for we all partake of the one bread. Behold Israel after the flesh;—are not they who eat the sacrifices *partners* of the altar? What do I say then? That an idol is anything, or a sacrifice offered to an idol is anything? No, I say that what the Gentiles sacrifice they sacrifice to devils and not to God, and I would not that you should be partners of devils. You cannot drink the cup of the Lord and the cup of devils; you cannot partake of the table of the Lord and of the table of devils." St Paul insists here upon seeing in a religious rite its proper spiritual significance. Give its due force to the feasting on a sacrifice, whether it be a Christian or a heathen sacrifice, and what must it mean? It brings you into union with the sacrifice and with the being to whom the sacrifice is offered. Every Jewish sacrifice, every heathen sacrifice, had equally the aim of bringing the worshippers into close union and partnership with the God worshipped. "How then," St Paul asks, "can you, who enter into union or fellowship with Christ in our Christian feast, allow yourselves to be similarly put into fellowship with false gods?"

Whenever the term Communion has been applied, in imitation of this example of St Paul, to the Lord's Supper, it has always been understood as having a twofold reference. It speaks first of a partaking of Christ or fellowship with Christ, and then of a mutual fellowship between those who are related in common to Christ. The double meaning flows obviously from the nature of the fact. Those who become respectively members of the same body become fellow-members, or members one of another. One bread, one cake, is divided into many parts, and given to many communicants; in partaking of the same bread they are associated together. Whatever creates a fellowship between each man and Christ, establishes a secondary bond of fellowship between all who have this union with Christ in common.

The subject of which I wish to speak chiefly under the head of Communion is the fellowship between man and man, confessed and proclaimed by all moralists, regarded by non-Christians as resting on various other grounds, but believed in by Christians, and set forth by the Holy Communion, as subsisting in the common relation of each to Christ. But something ought to be said first perhaps upon the question, What is it that constitutes the union of men with Christ? Does it originate in, or depend absolutely upon, a partaking of the Body and Blood of Christ in the Holy Communion?

Possibly some would answer that it does. But no Christian to whom Christian life is more than a name, whatever language he may use in obedience to the logic of a doctrinal theory or when he desires to do all the honour he can to a Divinely ordained Sacrament, has ever forced himself to speak always in consistency with such an answer. The affirmation, however rigorously intended, is always spoilt by exceptions. Christians believe in the Holy Spirit of God, breathing where he lists, a free mysterious subtle Spirit, infinite in grace as well as in power; and no one really dares to tie down the Divine Spirit absolutely to some visible and local vehicle. Nor is it possible for a Christian, believe as he may in some kind of corporeal feeding upon Christ, to think of a Communion so realized as higher in its nature than a Communion realized in the Spirit. There is not a hymn or prayer or meditation, accepted by Christians of any Church as an utterance of the deeper Christian feeling, in which Communion with Christ is not assumed to be essentially spiritual, possible at any time and in any place, and dependent ultimately on nothing but the eternal grace of God. The Holy Communion, therefore, with whatever truth its claims may be pressed as the legitimate channel of the grace of Communion, is not to be spoken of as the only mode of holding fellowship with Christ, nor even as the only mode of participating in his Body and Blood, so as to derive life from him. It is the obvious witness and pledge of such Communion; it is the appointed means of seeking it: but Christians do not feed on Christ exclusively in the Lord's Supper;—if it were so, the Sacrament would lose its own highest value. The worth of the Sacrament is that it expresses and brings home to us and stimulates that purely spiritual fellowship with Christ to which he himself invited his disciples, and on which he laid so much stress; it summons our spirits to active faith and love; it assures us of a presence and a support by which we may continually be saved. To attempt to do the Sacrament honour by making more of the flesh than of the Spirit is like insisting on the excellence of the paper of a bank-note and knowing nothing of its value as the representative of money.

Let it be observed that St Paul, in the passage quoted, treats the communion or partnership of idolaters with their false gods, and of members of Christ with one another, as of the same kind as the participating in the Body and Blood of Christ. All are examples of spiritual communion,—of a fellowship realized by the will, the affections, and the conscience. It would be well to bear in mind that, according to St Paul, the feeding together on the one Bread has the same kind of power to effect a mutual fellowship amongst ourselves, which it has to make us partakers of Christ. No one is in danger of saying that it is impossible for a man to hold communion with his fellow-Christians except in and through the Holy Communion; and it cannot be too strongly urged that it is the office of the Sacrament to bear witness to true human fellowship, and to pledge and help us to the fulfilment of it.

But when human fellowship is spoken of, the question is sure to arise in many minds, whether the communion of Christians with one another does not profess to be something essentially different from the bond which unites men as men together. This is a question upon which it is as easy to fall into mistakes as it is important to avoid them. Christian communion has undoubtedly some appearance of being exclusive; it has constantly been made exclusive in practice by Christians; excommunication, which is a term of the Christian Church, speaks of shutting out from a society. One of the most prominent features of Christian belief to many minds has been the doctrine, that the Church and the world,—or the society of believers and the rest of mankind,—are so entirely distinguished and separated from one another as to have almost nothing in common. Yet we habitually believe in a common humanity, as well as in the communion of the saints. Do these two kinds of fellowship belong to different spheres, or are they identical, or in what relation does each stand to the other?

The Catholic doctrine on this subject may, I think, be thus stated,—that *Christian Communion is natural human fellowship brought into the Divine light and quickened by the Divine Spirit.* Whatever binds men together is justified and raised to a higher power by the common union of men to a Divine Head. Let me offer some brief illustrations in support of this statement.

And, first, it is natural that we should look to Christ himself, and see what we may read in his life and words. The voice with which he speaks is too clear and emphatic to be misunderstood. It is equally recognized by believers and unbelievers. What is the title which he chooses for himself? That of *The Son of Man.* To us who behold in him the Son of God, it is a title glorious in its condescension and love, lifting up the whole human race, giving comfort and hope to every member of it. To others, it must surely seem a surprising pretension, in one who evidently knew so well the meaning of it; but they find in the actual truth of the pretension an explanation of the success of Jesus. The Son of Man! Whatever was human touched him, as it has touched no other; we are all less human than Christ. He loved and rejoiced and grieved, as one to whom every man was a dear brother. It was his peculiar witness and teaching, that even the evil were not to be shut out from the circle of kindly fellowship. "Be the children of your Father in heaven; for he maketh his sun to rise on the evil and on the good, and sendeth rain on the just and on the unjust." It was an accepted law amongst his countrymen, Thou shalt love thy neighbour as thyself: but narrow-minded Jews could fit it to their less human dispositions by asking, *But who is my neighbour?* Jesus replied by appealing to the simple instincts of humanity, and shewing how a Samaritan heretic might perfectly keep the law through natural kindness. The spirit in which he himself sympathized with sufferers made his followers see in him the fulfilment of the prophet's saying, "Himself took our infirmities and bare our sicknesses." He was capable indeed of terrible anger against men, but it was against men who in the name of God committed outrages on humanity. Those whom he repelled were the exclusive. When his denunciations were the hottest, his reproaches were such as these, "Ye lade men with burdens grievous to be borne, and ye yourselves touch not the burdens with one of your fingers." "Ye have taken away the key of knowledge: ye enter not in yourselves, and them that were entering in ye hindered." To Jesus Christ men as men were the children of his Father. To be humane was to be in sympathy with him; to be inhuman was to offend him and his Father.

Assuredly, if Christianity is to be studied first of all in Christ, it will be a difficult problem for either friend or enemy to draw a circle of Christian Communion leaving anything of humanity outside. The records of the life of Christ vindicate to the full his title of the Son of Man. When a thinker who is in perfect accord with modern ideas concerning humanity comes freshly to the examination of those records, he finds in Christ not the narrower affections of a less advanced civilization, but a richness and a warmth of human sympathy which place his life still before the largest-hearted man as a power and an example. The Son of Man, who healed in Galilee and thundered at Jerusalem, still claims the allegiance of Christendom.

But let us glance rapidly at the most ordinary causes by which human society is built up, and let us see how these are related to the principles of Christian fellowship.

Men are so made as to be dependent on one another. One wants what it is in the power of another to supply. The more completely men agree to help each other, the better off they all find themselves. So the operation of need and help tends perpetually to bind men together. But when we look to St Paul, for example, to see how he describes Christian fellowship, we observe that this relation is explicitly recognized and insisted upon. Christian society is a body, the members of which all have need of one another. The eye cannot say to the hand, I have no need of thee: nor again the head to the feet, I have no need of you. God has tempered the body together, compelling the more honourable parts to have due regard to the less honourable, so that the members should have the same care one for another. And whether one member suffer, all the members suffer with it; or one member be honoured, all the members rejoice with it. What theories of secular socialism can do anything more than imitate this ideal of St Paul's?

Again, there are social or sympathetic instincts in human nature which, apart from conscious wants, move men towards one another. The mutual love of husband and wife, of parents and children, the fraternal affections, the kindness of friends and neighbours, form the spiritual cement of every social system. What does Christian doctrine say to these natural bonds? I need hardly remind you how in the Christian system these sympathies are exalted and consecrated. They are the ligaments connecting the parts in the Divinely organized body, and enabling each to work in its place. The family, the city, the community, is a Divine creation. Such an aspect as that in which St Paul presents the duties of husband and wife may be mystical, may be called fanciful, but it undeniably tends to make those natural duties more sacred and binding. Husband and wife will not love each other less if they are true Christians, but more. If any Christian school has persuaded people that they ought, as heirs of heaven, to sit loose to natural affections, and has made the fulfilment of common relative obligations a mere condescension to the exigencies of a corrupt world, that is not Apostolical Christianity. In the days of the New Testament Christians were taught not to look down upon, but to reverence as Divine, the elementary bonds of human society.

Similarly, if we were to consider the common interests, common inheritances, common prospects, by which the citizens of a country are bound together, we should find that these, so far as they are worthy, are not only accepted, but lifted into a higher atmosphere, by the faith of the Christian. As we look back on history we say, "O God, we have heard with our ears, and our fathers have declared unto us, the noble works that thou didst in their days, and in the old time before them." That our country should be disgraced by crime and ignorance and social disorder causes in us a deeper grief and shame in proportion as we honour the Gospel and give God thanks for his grace. And when we are cherishing hope, what aim can we possibly have in the interest of society, which is not also an object of Christian prayer and Christian effort? Christianity indeed is far from sanctioning all that men do and seek; it has to condemn much of what goes on in the world: but, if any pursuit is really condemned by Christian doctrine, —by such doctrine, I mean, as that which we are reading in our Sacrament of Holy Communion,— we may be sure that such a pursuit is not thoroughly social, is not tending to build up society, but to dissolve and destroy it.

Let us look for a moment in this light at the causes which notoriously weaken and injure human fellowship. Is there one of these which Christianity encourages, which it does not expressly condemn? *Dishonesty*, for example, is always at its mischievous work, producing distrust between man and man. A man is tempted to suppress the truth, to utter a falsehood, to gain secretly some unfair advantage; whenever he yields to the temptation, society suffers. Dishonesty or falsehood is manifestly anti-social. But on that very account it is condemned by the Christian law. "Wherefore putting away lying," says St Paul, "speak every man truth with his neighbour; *for we are members one of another.*" How can fellow-members of the body of Christ do a thing so unnatural as to deceive one another? The mutual *jealousy*, again, which springs from irritated self-regard, is one of the great poisons of society. Beginning secretly, like a fatal gas, it broods and grows till some accident causes it to explode, with breaches and rents which can never be healed. But no one can come under the teaching of the Gospel without being distinctly warned, in the name of the Gospel, against the cherishing of resentment. The Gospel is the offer of forgiveness from God to men; but God's forgiveness, we are assured, cannot reach the unforgiving. "Forgive, and ye shall be forgiven." "If ye do not forgive, neither will your Father who is in heaven forgive you." "Be kind one to another, tenderhearted, forgiving one another, even as God in Christ has forgiven you." "Be angry and sin not; let not the sun go down upon your wrath, neither give place to the devil." "Give not room," that is, "for the dividing spirit, the spirit of misconstruction, of falsehood, of ill-will, to enter in and to set brother against brother." Another destroyer of the unity of society is *insolence*, the insolence of wealth and prosperity, the insolence of caste. What can strike more directly at the root of insolence than the law of Christ? "My brethren," says the Apostle, with grave remonstrance, "have not the faith of our Lord Jesus Christ, the Lord of glory, with respect of persons." "Who maketh thee to differ from another? and what hast thou that thou didst not receive? Now, if thou didst receive it, why dost thou glory, as if thou hadst not received it?" It is not to the New Testament that the rich man or the cultivated can go to find excuses for looking down upon the multitude. There, on the contrary, he will find incessant warnings as to his special dangers, and as to the retribution which will attend on his special sins. He will find the grace of God exalted above all worldly distinctions, and will be told that the poor have a better chance than he of receiving that grace... Or, take two opposite causes which introduce mischief into the economical system of society, *greed of money*, and *idleness*. A train of destructive influences proceed from both: from the eager love of money,—excessive speculation, hardness in driving bargains, overwork, a spirit of competition which looks on competitors as necessary enemies; from idleness,—a loose self-indulgence, neglect of relative obligations, a habit of fault-finding, poverty, pauperism. The law of Christ makes both covetousness and idleness offences against God. "Ye cannot serve God and Mammon." "Charge them that are rich in this world, that they be not high-minded nor trust in uncertain riches, but in the living God, who giveth us richly all things to enjoy; that they do good, that they be rich in good works, ready to distribute, willing to communicate." "As touching brotherly love, ye need not that I write unto you, for ye yourselves are taught of God to love one another. And indeed ye do it toward all the brethren which are in all Macedonia; but we beseech you, brethren, that ye increase more and more; and that ye study to be quiet and to do your own business, and to work with your own hands as we commanded you; that ye may walk honestly toward them that are without, and that ye may have lack of nothing." "Let a man labour, working with his hands the thing that is good, that he may have to give to him that needeth."

These are but examples of the way in which the true Christian faith meets every vice which threatens society, marks it with the more awful name of a sin against God, and charges men by their gratitude to God for his mercies and by their fear of his displeasure to avoid it and to war against it. Let a man be a true Christian, and he cannot do anything which he knows to be unsocial. To be in communion with Christ is to love God and man, and love, which works no ill to a neighbour, unconsciously fulfils the whole social law. "This is the message," says St John, "which we have heard from the Son of God and declare unto you, that God is light, and in him is no darkness at all. If we say that we have fellowship with him, and walk in darkness, we lie, and do not the truth: but if we walk in the light, as he is in the light, we have fellowship one with another." There is no room for doubt as to what St John meant by darkness and light. Light was love and righteousness; darkness was hatred and unrighteousness. The blessed revelation made by the coming of the Son of God in the flesh, was that God was perfectly righteous, perfectly loving, with a love and truth which could be known by humanity and reproduced by humanity. The eternal grounds of fellowship are righteousness and love. "We who were friends of the Lord Jesus," says St John, "declare to you what we have seen and heard, in order that you may have fellowship with us,—and our fellowship is with the Father and his Son Jesus Christ."

Certainly, these words themselves speak of a communion which is to be enjoyed by those who know and believe in Jesus Christ. Nothing that was said by any Apostle,—nothing, I hope, of what I have been saying,—can be rightly understood as implying that there is no such thing as a peculiar Christian fellowship. But the fellowship is of those who have learnt together that there is a hope for mankind which others have despaired of, or at which they have wistfully guessed; of those who have seen heaven opened and the Son of man standing on the right hand of God. This common faith cannot but make those who share it rejoice together and grieve together and labour together, till a fellow-feeling, a spiritual sympathy, of unbounded closeness and tenderness grows up between them. But the utmost growth of it does not separate them from their fellow-men, whatever belief and hopes these others may be entertaining; they love not the man the less, because they love the fellow-Christian the more. The exclusiveness which has been charged upon Christians has a twofold explanation. It may be the name for the fact that the strongest believers in Christ have set the highest value on the Gospel, and have desired most earnestly that all men should receive it, and have taken pains to guard their own faith and love from growing cold, and have assumed that not to be a Christian was to be suffering a loss beyond calculation. I have been quoting St John; and it is probable that no one, after reading his Epistles, would be inclined to claim St John as a Liberal. But there is another kind of exclusiveness, belonging to Christians but not to Christianity; due to the forgetting of St John's great lesson, that the Revelation we have received is a manifestation of God in his Son as infinitely righteous and good. Christians who fence themselves off from their fellow-men are offenders against the law of humanity; but they are first of all disloyal to the law of Christ. There is no danger of Christians clinging to one another too closely, so long as they are bound together in the common love of the Son of man.

When at first the new fervour of humanity was stirring in the Christian body, it had two principal triumphs: it brought rich and poor into sincere fellowship; and it constrained Jews to acknowledge men of other races as brethren. If a more lively spirit of communion, derived from fellowship with Christ, were to be aroused amongst ourselves, it would assuredly find work of both kinds to do. On the binding of rich and poor together, though modern circumstances might suggest much to say, I will only say this: that the power of Christian principle to adjust classes together, making them helpful and not hostile to each other, must come from the recognition of men, both rich and poor, as brethren in God's family; not from the exaggerated estimate of the value of riches and power, and of the rights of the poor to attain a share in them, but from a confession that all are cared for by God, all are responsible to him, and that it is an infinitely more important question whether a man is just and merciful, a true man, honouring all men, than whether he is rich or poor, great or small. On the *Catholic* influence of Christian communion or its power to obliterate the isolation of races, I am tempted to dwell a little longer, because we in England have been charged with making patriotic isolation a virtue, and high-minded men, like the authors of the Essays on International Policy, have set themselves to rebuke our pride of race, and to urge upon Englishmen their obligations as members of the great human family. It has been represented by our most eloquent statesman and repeated by others*, that those who have laboured most zealously to promote freedom of trade, did not so earnestly desire to increase wealth at home, as to bring about what they held to be a far higher end, a more cordial international fellowship. Now particular accusations of unjust and selfish and insolent disregard of human rights should be tested by facts: but if we have to plead guilty, we surely have in our New Testament, in our Creeds and Prayers, a more direct and forcible condemnation than can light on us from any other quarter. If the obligations of humanity between different races of men have indeed to be brought before us as a discovery of our age, why have we been for so many generations professing to be Catholic Christians? Let us be thankful for modern lessons, modern reproofs: but let us take to ourselves the deeper shame, when we remember to what sacred teaching we must have made ourselves deaf. We belong to the Church of St Peter, to whom God shewed that he should not call any man common or unclean; of St Paul, who saw that membership in Christ transcended all distinctions of Jew and Greek, barbarian, Scythian, bond and free; of St John, who had visions of a great multitude, of all nations and kindreds and people and tongues, standing before the throne and

---

* Richard Cobden's aims have been thus described by Mr Gladstone, Lord Hobart, and others.

before the Lamb, and of a New Jerusalem into which the glory and honour of the nations were to be brought. We read perhaps many times in the year that broadest of statements, made by a Christian Apostle pleading with a heathen audience: "God hath made of one blood all nations of men, for to dwell on all the face of the earth; and hath determined the times before appointed and the bounds of their habitation; that they should seek the Lord, if haply they might feel after him and find him, though he be not far from every one of us: for in him we live and move and have our being; as certain also of your own poets have said, For we are also his offspring." This is the creed of Christians as to Englishmen and Frenchmen, as to Indians and Negroes.

With reference to the relations of commerce to the cordial human intercourse of different nations, we might challenge any modern politician to state those relations more thoroughly or more beautifully than they were stated 300 years ago in the simple language of Catholic Christianity by one of our English rulers. I quote from a letter sent by Edward VIth with an expedition of discovery, and addressed to the rulers of any country at which the expedition might arrive: "Forasmuch as the great and Almighty God hath given unto mankind, above all other living creatures, such an heart and desire, that every man desireth to join friendship with other, to love and be loved, also to give and receive mutual benefits: it is therefore the duty of all men according to their power to maintain and increase this desire in every man, with well deserving to all men, and especially to shew this good affection to such as being moved with this desire come to them from far countries....For the God of heaven and earth, greatly providing for mankind, would not that all things should be found in one region, to the end that one should have need of another, that by this means friendship might be established among all men, and every one seek to gratify all. For the furtherance of which universal amity, certain men of our realm, moved hereunto by the said desire, have instituted and taken upon them a voyage into far countries, desiring us to further their enterprise. Who, assenting to their petition, have licensed the right valiant and worthy Sir Hugh Willoughby, Kt. and others our trusty and faithful servants, to go to countries to them heretofore unknown, as well to seek such things as we lack, as also to carry unto them from our regions such things as they lack. So that hereby not only commodity may ensue both to them and us, but also an indissoluble and perpetual league of friendship be established between us both. We therefore desire you kings and princes and all other to whom there is any power on the earth, to permit unto these our servants free passage by your regions and dominions; for they shall not touch anything of yours unwilling unto you. *Consider you that they also are men.* If therefore they shall stand in need of anything, we desire you of all humanity and for the nobility which is in you to aid and help them with such things as they lack, receiving again of them such things as they shall be able to give you in recompense. Shew yourselves so towards them, as you would that we and our subjects should shew ourselves towards your servants, if at any time they shall pass by our regions*."—That, I repeat, is the theory of trade according to Catholic Christianity. It may be a reproach to us if we have to learn a poor imitation of it from some other teachers, but the reproach ought not to fall on the Gospel to which through our narrowness we have been unfaithful.

To sum up in a few concluding words what I have been endeavouring to set before you.—Our Holy Communion preaches that through fellowship with Christ our Divine Head we have fellowship with one another. There are two ways in which this preaching may be set at nought. We may exalt the Sacrament, but by making it magical instead of spiritual, we may forfeit its moral influence. Or, we may fix our thoughts respectfully on human fellowship, but resolve to shut out the idea of any Divine bond of it. In the contemplation of the former of these tendencies I would urge, *Consider* the Sacrament which you honour: let it teach you, as it will, the sacredness of common humanity. With those who may be affected by the latter I would plead, Is not human fellowship illustrated and consecrated and bound home upon the consciences of men, by the acknowledgment of the Son of Man, who is the Head of every man? Without Christ, you either lose the immense help of an ideal in which even corrupt and offensive humanity has an admitted claim upon you; or you set up an ideal which you know to be your own invention. How can the best and highest be persuaded,—not to *patronize* humanity, but to serve it in all humility, unless they see behind the foolish and perishing races of mankind the abiding Figure of the Divine Man?

It would not be right, indeed, to take up a faith in Christ merely because the acknowledgment of him would be good for human fellowship. But we may rightly use the contemplation of this fact, if it be one, to support and vitalize our faith. Is there not a region, an atmosphere, into which both our religion and our ordinary conceptions of life need equally to rise? We are brought up to believe in a spiritual world, in which God and Christ and the living spirits of men who toil and who endure are the realities. Is it possible that well-meaning persons should be tempted in our generation to decline from that faith, to seek life and comfort either in the weak and beggarly rudiments of ceremonial observance, or in the laws and interests of a world without Christ? Let us listen rather to the high-toned appeal, "Stand fast in the liberty with which Christ has made us free." Having begun in the Spirit, are we now to be made perfect by the flesh?—God forbid!